Youth & Parents Together

Facing Life's Struggles

Leaders Guide
13-Week Curriculum for Junior High Kids and Their Parents

. . . .

By Mike Gillespie

Loveland, Colorado

Facing Life's Struggles: Leaders Guide

Copyright © 1988 by Mike Gillespie
First Printing

Credits
Edited by Nancy M. Shaw
Designed by Judy Atwood

Scripture quotations are from the Holy Bible, New International Version. Copyright © 1973, 1978, 1984 International Bible Society. Used by permission of Zondervan Bible Publishers.

ISBN 0931-529-27-1

Printed in the United States of America

Contents

Introduction

Facing Life's Struggles can transform and energize family relationships; it can build communication channels and enhance spiritual growth. *Facing Life's Struggles* is a 13-week curriculum for junior highers and their parents that includes many active ideas for sharing and interaction. The sessions are built on a solid biblical foundation and written as a journey of faith for everyone involved.

Questions About the Study

1. Why try a curriculum for both parents and junior highers? Bleak statistics scare us with the fact that the family unit is in trouble. Even when churches provide nurturing opportunities for Christian growth in the family, the approach often segregates families—parents participate in one class, kids participate in another.

Facing Life's Struggles offers parents and junior highers a chance to study together and discover new openness and appreciation for each other. What better place to do this than in the arena of God's loving support?

Facing Life's Struggles strengthens the family through a creative, active, interesting, challenging process of discovery. Families openly communicate their faith and personal opinions. The sharing process cultivates strong bonds between parents and junior highers.

2. What do parents and junior highers have in common to study for 13 weeks? A lot! The themes explored in this curriculum are expressly designed for parent and child interaction. Parents of junior highers find their lives in transition. Parents re-examine those same hard questions of adolescence. Topics like winning, forgiveness, anger, faith, loneliness, persecution, patience, trust, compassion, fear, doubt, discouragement, temptation, communication and God's promises are powerful issues for discussion.

Adults and young people will surprise each other on how much alike they are. Each generation faces the same issues and problems.

When parents and junior highers share their thoughts and feelings about stimulating themes of faith, Christian education journeys into a new and powerful dimension.

3. Will junior highers and parents both benefit from this curriculum? Dramatically! Young people desperately need a forum for questioning and communication. They harbor intense feelings of insecurity. Creating an environment where adults share their faith and become "real people" powerfully benefits young adolescents. Junior highers receive (and give!) a new sense of direction as they wrestle with faith issues where God's promises are shared and affirmed. Families are strengthened tremendously by the educational designs that encourage discussion and interaction. The wisdom of caring, loving adults provides a nurturing influence on young, searching minds.

Adults benefit as they share their feelings about significant life issues. Creative exchanges with vibrant junior highers energize parents' tired and sore emotional muscles. Discoveries about their young people open new vistas for understanding and make the adolescent years an unlimited opportunity for exciting parenthood.

4. What if I have an extra small group—or an extra large group? These sessions can be completed with any size group. When directions call for participants to divide into small groups, groups with 10 participants or fewer would simply complete the activity together. Larger groups would follow the directions and duplicate activities and supplies when necessary.

5. Are these sessions designed for "traditional" (Mom, Dad and kid) families only? Single-parent, blended and foster families as well as traditional families should participate in the study. The goal is to develop open communication between parents and junior highers, no matter what their situation.

6. Must participants attend every session? Although it is best for families to attend all sessions, they will not fall behind if they can't attend each one.

On some occasions, a parent may not be able to attend,

but the junior higher can—or vice versa. That's okay. Be aware of this possibility and plan for it. When an activity calls for family units to gather, you can pair up with the solo junior higher or with the solo parent. Or you can plan for "foster families" and ask the participant to join another family unit for the session. Encourage the solo participant to go over the session with the absent family members sometime during the following week.

The Sessions

As a teacher, you may feel apprehensive as you prepare to lead this 13-week study. (Most teachers have these feelings even after years of experience.) Put your mind at ease about the curriculum you will teach. The Leaders Guide contains all the necessary tools for building exciting, stimulating studies for your participants. Comprehensive session outlines offer an array of sound, practical, educational activities that *involve* the participants in the study.

Each session of the curriculum is built on the following five parts that allow for maximum dissection of the theme and create lively interaction:

Opening—an activity, game, discussion or project to warm up participants. The activities prepare the participants to open up for quality communication.

Theme presentation—a brief time to describe the session's theme and whet participants' enthusiasm.

Exploration—role plays, monologues, readings, simulation games, collages, worksheets and other varied activities used to explore the topic.

Response—a time for participants to think about what they've learned and apply it to their lives.

Closing affirmation—a time for family members to affirm each other. (This important aspect often is overlooked in families' busy schedules.)

Varied activities are used to explore the topics each week, but these five segments remain constant from session to session. This basic consistency brings depth and continuity to the curriculum and increases the effectiveness of your teaching.

Each session is based on a 55-minute time frame. Suggested times for each of the five segments are included;

however, occasions may arise when you will want to alter these. Be responsive to special moments of sharing.

These sessions can be easily lengthened by allowing more time for discussion on each question and participation in each activity. Likewise, the session can be shortened by choosing questions you would most like to discuss, or by deleting a worksheet from the class time and asking families to complete it at home. Feel free to adapt the time segments to your own needs.

In addition to the session elements obvious to the participants, the Leaders Guide provides the following teacher supports for each session:

Objectives—short, concise statements about what participants will do and learn.

Biblical Foundation—Bible verses relating to the week's theme.

Background for Leader—additional, helpful information for the leader to prepare.

Preparation—detailed list of necessary materials and guidelines.

"Table Talk" Section

One of the important ingredients of this curriculum is the "Table Talk" section. "Table Talk" allows families a chance to continue the communication that started during each session. By discussing issues in the privacy of the home, greater discoveries can take place and families can grow closer. Here are some suggestions for helping the "Table Talk" time become a regular weekly process for your participants:

1. Ask family members to covenant for a time together before they leave the classroom. They can write their time and day in the box on the "Table Talk" worksheet for each session. If each family member does this, he or she will feel committed to save that time for the family.

2. Check informally with participants at the beginning of each class to get feedback on their "Table Talk" experiences.

3. Set up an informal lunch after church once a month during the 13-week study and invite participants to stay and conduct their "Table Talk" sessions then. This would give you a chance to participate and interact with families.

Gather groups at the end to share insights.

4. Ask families to encourage all members to participate in "Table Talk." Brothers and sisters of all ages can also benefit from the experiences.

5. Ask families to tell you about their "Table Talk" time each week by completing a simple form like the following one. Assure families you are not trying to snoop, but are looking for ways to provide support. Keep track of issues that surface during discussions and elaborate on them in class.

"Table Talk" Progress for the week of

_____

Our topic this week was:

We spent most of our time focusing on:

We agreed on:

We disagreed on:

The best thing that happened this week was:

Some of the goals we set for our family are:

Distribute these forms at the end of each session and collect them when families return the following week. As families get to know one another, they may feel comfortable about posting their forms so others can share in their progress. This would increase the level of sharing and commitment to one another. It would also encourage less-involved participants to approach the class at a deeper level.

"Table Talk" is important. Positive growth can come from this experience. It's also a positive way to keep parents and young people talking to each other.

Participants Books

Participants Books ease and facilitate your preparation time since each Participants Book includes all worksheets and ''Table Talk'' sections. The sessions begin with a brief introduction followed by the specific learning objectives.

For the first session, gather one Participants Book for each person. Keep a few extra books in case some people join the class later. Encourage people to take home their books each week to complete their ''Table Talk'' time, and remind them to bring the books back to the next session. If people forget, let them use one of your extras for that session.

Clues for an Effective Study

1. Communicate. Send a letter to all junior highers and their parents before the curriculum starts. Outline the unique nature of the approach and invite families to commit to this stimulating 13-week study. For example, you can send a letter similar to the following page.

2. Publicize. Publicize the study throughout your church. Create excitement for the study through creative letters, posters, fliers and bulletin inserts. Ask a parent and junior higher to present a skit during announcement time at church.

3. Choose the right meeting area. Arrange for a comfortable meeting area that will allow for small group mobility and activities. Cramped quarters will quickly erode enthusiasm and attendance.

4. Try co-teaching. Teach the curriculum with another person. Two people leading the sessions will make them more exciting and energetic. It is also more fun for two people to plan together and share teaching responsibilities.

5. Be organized. Always review each session thoroughly. Highlight the topics, questions and activities that you want most to cover. Although all worksheets are included in the Participants Book, additional supplies will be needed. Prepare those ahead of time. Avoid last-minute scurrying for supplies. Preparation gives you confidence for moving smoothly from one activity to another.

6. Start on time. Covenant with your class members to be prompt in their attendance. Start at the set time. Failure to do this only gives people permission to be late. Each

Sample Letter

Dear Parents and Junior Highers:

As you know, our church believes that family relation-ships are important. So, we're offering a chance for you to strengthen your relationships with each other.

Beginning Sunday, January 15, we'll offer a 13-week study titled *Facing Life's Struggles*. The meetings will be fun, activity-packed and meaningful. Each week, we'll talk about topics that affect both junior highers and parents such as fear, doubt, discouragement, loneliness, faith, impatience, anger, persecution, temptation, being a winner, forgiveness, trust, compassion, communication and God's promises.

We'll meet at the education center from 9:00-9:55 a.m. from January 15 through April 8.

Gather your family members and commit to this study. Read the following Family Covenant, then have each member sign it. Cut along the dotted line and return the covenant to the church office by January 3.

God's blessings to you and your family!

Sincerely,

Susan

Susan Pearson
Youth Minister

- -

Family Covenant

We promise to complete this 13-week study, to arrive promptly to each session, and to complete all assignments together.

As a family, we pledge to be open, honest and compas-sionate with each other as we communicate and grow spiritually.

Family members: _____

_____

_____

_____

session is filled with educational activities. Cutting the class time short will prevent potential discoveries.

7. Meet with parents. At the end of the first session, meet privately for a few moments with the parents. Explain the unique approach of the coming weeks. Encourage them to be supportive and patient with the junior highers. Remind them to listen to the young people in the group, especially their own children. Discourage the tendency to dominate small group discussions. Challenge parents to do whatever is necessary to draw the young people into conversations during class time.

Talk about the need for openness and honesty. Encourage parents to be open to change and growth in their own faith. Open their eyes to the possibilities for deepening family relationships and understanding.

Encourage a strong commitment to follow through with the "Table Talk" sessions each week. Inform them that the pace of these sessions will be faster than what they might be accustomed to in adult educational settings. The quicker pace reflects the need to reach junior highers.

8. Be adaptable. If you find a process is not working during class, glean what you can and move on. The number of activities allows for some flexibility, but they are also designed to build on one another. Be cautious not to pick only those particular activities you want to use. Arbitrarily excluding some activities may stifle the opportunities for discovery. Use your best judgment, however, since ultimately you know what will work best for your class.

9. Be open. Expect miracles of faith and family nurture to take place. Allow God to use you as an agent of grace. Share your leadership in such a way that you bring care and support to all class members. Pray for your class constantly.

10. Understand junior highers. Be mindful of the peculiarities of junior high young people. They are active, spontaneous and sometimes sultry. They need quick movement from one educational process to another to make learning challenging, fun and effective. For this reason you will find a potpourri of approaches in the curriculum.

Be patient with your junior highers when they don't respond. Be generous in your praise when they do. Accept the ways they share as gifts of self-expression. Temper their occasional cynical nature with a big dose of encouragement and affirmation.

11. Be creative. Use several of the sessions for a family weekend retreat. Combine a couple of sessions for an overnight lock-in. Use the 13 weeks of ideas as Sunday school material, or use them for a weekly family night. The possibilities are endless!

12. Have fun! Although you will be leading the sessions, you will learn much from the parents and junior highers. Enjoy the participants and enjoy the activities.

Crippled by Fear, Doubt and Discouragement

Fear, doubt and discouragement influence everyone and come in various sizes. They can devastate junior highers and cripple adults. Family members can learn how to deal with these negative influences and how to provide understanding, affirmation and support for each other. Recognizing God's presence in each other's lives brings hope, strength and confidence for coping with these heavy loads.

This session explores the difficult times when discouragement fills a family's life. Biblical explorations affirm the good news that God never gives up on anyone and better days are ahead.

Objectives

During this session participants will:

● identify and talk to each other about their fears, doubts and discouragements.

● look at Peter's life as an example of someone who faced similar problems.

● list ways they can help each other conquer these negative influences in their lives.

● identify scripture passages which offer hope and strength.

Biblical Foundation

Peter's life:

Matthew 4:18-22; 8:14-17; 10:1-15; 14:22-36; 16:13-28; 17:1-13; 18:21-22; 26:30-46, 69-75

Mark 1:16-20, 29-34; 8:27-30; 9:2-13; 14:27-31, 66-72

Luke 4:38-41; 5:1-11; 9:18-21, 28-36; 22:31-34, 54-62

John 18:1-11, 15-18; 20:1-10; 21:15-19
Relating to fear: Psalm 23
Jesus faced doubts in the wilderness: Matthew 4:1-11
Jesus' disciples showed wavering faith: Matthew 8:23-27
People doubted Jesus' power: Matthew 9:23-26
Jesus faced discouragement: Matthew 13:53-58
Jesus experienced fear: Matthew 26:39
Relating to doubt: Romans 8:37-39
Relating to discouragement: Philippians 4:10-13

Background for Leader

Young adolescents are vulnerable to fear, doubt and discouragement as they struggle toward self-discovery. They need to find hope in the midst of this pressure to discover who they are apart from their parents. Parents also face similar struggles. When parents fail to resolve the search for personal identity as teenagers, they continue this struggle as adults. Sharing one another's personal fears, doubts and discouragements is healing for both parents and their children. Both groups can grow to understand each other and cope more effectively with these struggles in family life.

Peter is an example of someone who struggled with powerful moments of fear, doubt and discouragement. Yet Jesus never gave up on him. Jesus never dismissed Peter from his group of disciples. Gently, but firmly, Jesus helped Peter deal with his fears and doubts.

Preparation

Gather Bibles, scissors, pencils, markers, masking tape, newsprint and one Participants Book for each person. Prepare extra copies of the "Certificates of Appreciation" if you have any families who will have more than four people in attendance.

Make four large letters (A, B, C, D) on newsprint and tape these in the four corners of the room. Tape two sheets of newsprint on the front wall. Place a marker nearby. Tape three large sheets of newsprint on the other three walls. Write the words "Fear," "Doubt" and "Discouragement"— one on each sheet. Arrange the chairs in a semicircle facing the front of the room.

Ask a church member to play the part of Peter. Explain that he will come to class dressed like a *contemporary* fisherman. For example, he could wear waders and carry a fishing pole. Ask this person to memorize "Peter's Monologue," not read it. Remind him to emphasize Peter's times of fear, doubt and discouragement and Peter's amazement that Jesus never gave up on him despite his faults.

Ask another adult to interrupt your introduction of the theme at the appropriate time so you can introduce Peter.

(If you have difficulty finding someone to play Peter's part, record the monologue on tape ahead of time and play it for the group as if it were a recorded letter from the past. Ask everyone to listen carefully and take notes.)

Session

Opening (5 minutes)—Welcome all junior highers and parents to the course. Explain: "Over the next 13 weeks we'll discuss a number of topics that affect all families: loneliness, faith, impatience, anger, persecution, temptations, forgiveness, trust, compassion and communication. Today's session focuses on fear, doubt and discouragement.

"Everyone will receive a Participants Book to use throughout this study. The books are filled with worksheets to complete during each session and questions to discuss as a family after each session. Help each other remember to bring back the book each time we meet."

Gather everyone into the center of the room for the opening activity. Point out the large letters in the corners of the room. Tell the group: "One at a time, I'll ask five questions and you'll indicate your answers by moving to one of the corners. You'll have a short time to explain your response before I continue. I'll raise my hand when I'm ready to read the next question." Ask the following questions:

1. If there has ever been a time in your life when you were afraid of the dark, go to corner A. If you have never been afraid of the dark, go to corner B. Share with one other person why you were afraid or why you weren't.

Peter's Monologue

Hello, my name is Peter. I'm a fisherman. Thanks for inviting me to come today and tell about my experiences with Jesus.

My story began beside the Sea of Galilee. It was just another day. My brother Andrew and I were bringing in the boat when we saw this man standing on the shore. There was a presence about him I couldn't explain.

He walked over to our boat and told us to come and follow him. He wanted us to help him "fish" for people. What he said sounded pretty silly. In fact, Andrew and I looked at each other and laughed halfheartedly, but we found ourselves drawn to him. My life was never the same after that day. My family could never understand how I could wander off that way until the day Jesus healed my mother-in-law's fever. At that point they began to comprehend the impact this man had made on my life.

Jesus called 12 of us to walk with him. We were a mixed lot, including a tax collector and some simple fishermen. I still don't know why he wanted me in that group. I was impatient. I'd always had trouble controlling my temper or saying things I shouldn't. I certainly wasn't polished in dealing with other human beings, but he called me anyway. At that time none of us realized we were walking in the presence of God's Son.

I learned so much during those three years. I saw Jesus do things no one was supposed to be able to do. He cast out demons. He brought sight to blind people and made crippled people walk. He touched lepers and never caught the disease. Sinners changed when they came into his presence. Everything he did communicated his love to people.

I remember many "down" times as well as happy times—like that late night on the Sea of Galilee when Jesus came walking to us across the water. At first I wasn't sure who he was. I yelled, "Lord, if it's you, help me come to you on the water."

He simply said, "Come."

Without thinking, I stepped out of the boat. I kept looking at him as I walked across the water. I was fine until the wind began to blow and the waves began to slap at my knees. Then I looked around and was afraid. When I started to sink, I cried out, "Save me, Jesus!" He simply reached out his hand and pulled me to safety. All I did was take my eyes off him, and that made all the difference.

There was also that powerful night when Jesus asked us who we thought he was. The others thought he was a prophet or Elijah. I knew Jesus was more than a prophet or Elijah, but I was afraid to respond. Finally, he looked straight into my eyes and asked, "Who do you say I am?"

Through my tears, I looked into his loved-filled face and said, "You are the Christ, the Son of the living God." At that moment a powerful warmth came over me. When Jesus told us he was going to build his church on that response, I was overwhelmed. Me, Peter, a simple fisherman! He was going to build his church on me!

Later, when Jesus began to talk to us about his having to die, I tried to argue with him. When he became angry with me, I became even more confused because I didn't understand what he was trying to say. But when I looked at him, I realized he wasn't lying. After that experience, I didn't want to talk about his death anymore. It was just too frightening to think about.

Jesus continued to talk to us about God—about God's love for each one of us and how we could share that love with one another. His message motivated us to want to reach out to everyone. We just couldn't keep our feelings in. I watched him perform miracle after miracle in numerous crowds. I saw how he loved the people and how they loved him back. But there was always that other group, lurking around, trying to find some way to trip him up. I began to dislike them intensely.

I remember distinctly the last time we walked into Jerusalem together. I had dreaded this particular celebration because Jesus said he would never leave the city alive. That night before we ate our last meal together, Jesus took the basin and towel of a servant and washed every person's feet. I could hardly stand it—Jesus, the Son of God, washing my feet! It should have been *me* with that basin washing *his* feet. How could he do that for me?

After we had eaten, Jesus added to my discomfort by telling me I would deny him that night. I was hurt by his accusation. I knew he had to be wrong. Later when we went to the garden to pray with him, none of us could stay awake. Suddenly, that other group was on us, led by Judas, our own companion. When I used my sword to defend Jesus against these intruders, he stopped me. Then he just walked away with them.

That night I wandered the streets—alone, confused, hurt and dazed. Then someone shouted: "Hey, there's one of the men that was with that guy Jesus. Let's arrest him."

"No, no," I said, "I don't know him!" In that brief instant, I denied the most important person in the world to me. Later on, the shouts came again, and twice more I denied knowing him. When dawn broke and the rooster crowed to greet the new day, I fell down and wept in shame.

After days of political juggling, the other group hanged him on that cross and murdered him. He didn't fight back. He even forgave them for what they were doing while he suffered a miserable death. Everything seemed so final. Three years were gone! What were all those years about?

Eleven of us huddled in that upstairs room. Our lives had been ripped apart. It seemed there was nothing to do but go back to our boats and the lives we had left behind. Suddenly, Mary burst into the room crying, "The tomb is empty!"

John and I ran as fast as we could. The tomb was empty! Jesus was gone! Then we remembered his confusing promise that on the third day he would rise from the dead. It was true!

Later on, when Jesus came to see us, I was terrified and ashamed to face him. But he looked at me with those same loving eyes and asked, "Peter, do you love me?" Of course I did; I'd wanted to apologize a hundred times. He just smiled at me and said, "Peter, feed my sheep."

When the Holy Spirit came in Jesus' place, I understood what he meant by that statement. There was work to be done, people to see and lives to change. I realized that even when I had struggled with my fears, doubts and discouragements, Jesus continued to love me. Even when I denied him, he stuck with me. He never said I wasn't good enough to be part of his plan. I never got tired of talking about this man Jesus. You see, he never gave up on me.

2. If there has ever been a time when you were discouraged about school, go to corner C. If you have never been discouraged about school, go to corner D. If you are an adult, share the reason for your choice with a young person in your group. If you are a young person, share the reason for your choice with an adult in your group.

3. If there has ever been a time when you doubted God, go to corner B. If you have never doubted God, go to corner A. Share your reason with one other person in your group.

4. If there has ever been a time when you were afraid of your parents, go to corner D. If you have never been afraid of your parents, go to corner C. Go around the group and ask each person to make a one-sentence statement about that fear.

5. If there has ever been a time when you doubted your worth as a person, go to corner A. If you have never doubted your worth as a person, go to corner B. Share your feelings with one other group member.

Use additional questions if you have time.

Theme presentation (10 minutes)—Ask everyone to sit in the chairs. Talk briefly about the theme for today—the issues of fear, doubt and discouragement. Remind the group that everyone faces these times; no one is immune.

(Ask the adult to interrupt your meeting with a whispered message at this time.)

Tell the group you invited a special visitor to your meeting and you have just been informed that he's here. (On that cue, Peter enters the room.) Introduce Peter and tell the group you have invited the apostle to share his life's journey. Turn the meeting over to Peter to present his dramatic monologue.

Exploration (20 minutes)—Ask the class to share some things they have just discovered about Peter. Record their responses on the newsprint you taped to the front wall. Ask the group:

1. What affected you most about Peter's life?
2. How was Peter's life typical of your own?
3. What are some issues Peter faced that you struggle with today?

Break into small groups, mixing young people and

Peter's Experiences

Instructions: As a small group, read the different scripture passages aloud. In the box under each scripture passage, create a symbol to remind you of what you have just read. For example, when you read the passage about Peter walking on the water you could symbolize Peter's doubt by drawing waves with a question mark walking on the water. Write answers to the questions that follow each passage. Share your symbols and discuss the questions within your small group.

Peter Doubts

"Lord, if it's you," Peter replied, "tell me to come to you on the water."

"Come," he said.

Then Peter got down out of the boat, walked on the water and came toward Jesus. But when he saw the wind, he was afraid and, beginning to sink, he cried out, "Lord, save me!"

Immediately Jesus reached out his hand and caught him. "You of little faith," he said, "why did you doubt?" (Matthew 14:28-31).

1. How does this symbol help you remember how Jesus responds to doubt?

2. What does Jesus' response mean for you and other people today?

Peter Fears

Now Peter was sitting out in the courtyard, and a servant girl came to him. "You also were with Jesus of Galilee," she said.

But he denied it before them all. "I don't know what you're talking about," he said.

Then he went out to the gateway, where another girl saw him and said to the people there, "This fellow was with Jesus of Nazareth."

He denied it again, with an oath: "I don't know the man!"

After a little while, those standing there went up to Peter and said, "Surely you are one of them, for your accent gives you away."

Then he began to call down curses on himself and he swore to them, "I don't know the man!"

Immediately a rooster crowed (Matthew 26:69-74).

1. How can this symbol help you remember Peter's response to fear?

2. When was a time fear made you do something you didn't want to do?

Peter Gets Discouraged

When he had finished speaking, he said to Simon, "Put out into deep water, and let down the nets for a catch."

Simon answered, "Master, we've worked hard all night and haven't caught anything. But because you say so, I will let down the nets" (Luke 5:4-5).

1. How can this symbol help you remember how Peter responded to Jesus' directions?

2. What did Peter's answer mean to you?

After you have completed this worksheet, turn immediately to the "Personal Vessels of Fear, Doubt and Discouragement" worksheet and follow directions carefully.

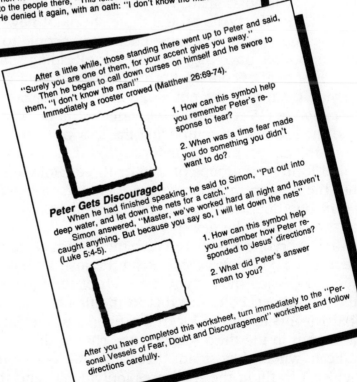

adults. Go around the room and have the young people say fear, doubt or discouragement—one at a time, in that order. Then ask the parents to do the same. Assign a location to each of the three groups.

Pass a Participants Book and a pencil to each person. Have everyone write his or her name in the front of the book. Ask everyone to turn to the worksheet titled "Peter's Experiences." Ask the groups to follow along as you read the instructions. Remind the groups to take turns reading the scripture passages aloud. Ask them to allow time for individuals to draw their symbols and answer the questions on paper before discussing them in the group.

As the groups complete this worksheet, remind them to move immediately to the "Personal Vessels of Fear, Doubt and Discouragement" worksheet. As you pass out scissors, markers and masking tape to each group, explain that individuals should write in each boat something in their lives which currently fits under each category of fear, doubt or discouragement. After they have finished writing, they should cut their boats apart, tear off a small strip of masking tape and tape their boats on the three sheets of newsprint under the appropriate headings. Encourage people to read others' responses once they are finished. Reading similar responses should encourage both parents and young people and assure them they are not alone in their struggles.

Response (15 minutes)—Individuals will be wandering around the room after completing the task of taping their boats to the newsprint. Ask them to find their family members and form new groups of two or three family units. Within the new small groups, have each person describe one fear, one doubt or one discouragement from the boats he or she taped to the newsprint.

After everyone has shared, ask the groups to turn to the "Where Are You?" worksheet. Read the instructions together and explain the activity for each of the three sections on the worksheet. Point out that in the first two sections the participants merely color in the figures to indicate their position, but in the third section they should draw a person to indicate where they stand. If there are no questions, ask participants to fill in the responses individually and then share responses within their family groups.

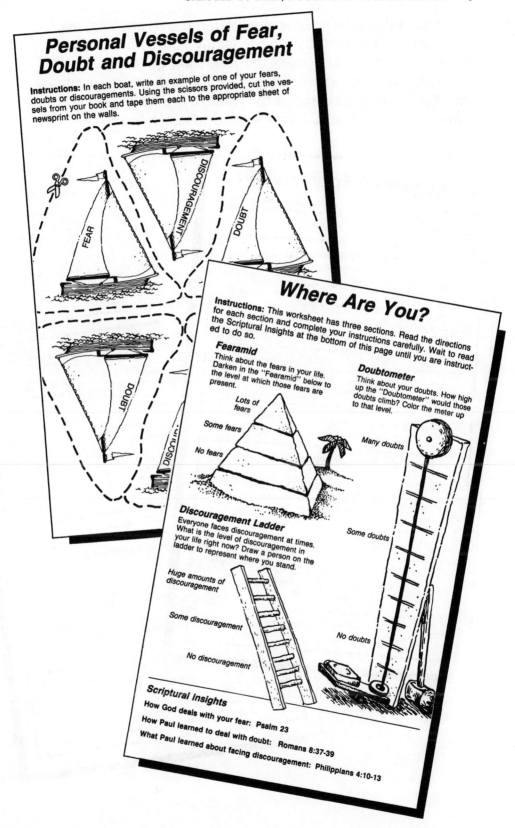

Personal Vessels of Fear, Doubt and Discouragement

Instructions: In each boat, write an example of one of your fears, doubts or discouragements. Using the scissors provided, cut the vessels from your book and tape them each to the appropriate sheet of newsprint on the walls.

FEAR

DISCOURAGEMENT

DOUBT

DOUBT

DISCOUR

Where Are You?

Instructions: This worksheet has three sections. Read the directions for each section and complete your instructions carefully. Wait to read the Scriptural Insights at the bottom of this page until you are instructed to do so.

Fearamid
Think about the fears in your life. Darken in the "Fearamid" below to the level at which those fears are present.

Lots of fears

Some fears

No fears

Doubtometer
Think about your doubts. How high up the "Doubtometer" would those doubts climb? Color the meter up to that level.

Many doubts

Some doubts

No doubts

Discouragement Ladder
Everyone faces discouragement at times. What is the level of discouragement in your life right now? Draw a person on the ladder to represent where you stand.

Huge amounts of discouragement

Some discouragement

No discouragement

Scriptural Insights
How God deals with your fear: Psalm 23

How Paul learned to deal with doubt: Romans 8:37-39

What Paul learned about facing discouragement: Philippians 4:10-13

After most groups have completed the worksheet, ask everyone to stay with his or her family and come to the front of the room to discuss the following questions:

1. As parents, how did you feel about the fears, doubts and discouragements shared by your young people? Were you surprised? What did you want to do in response to

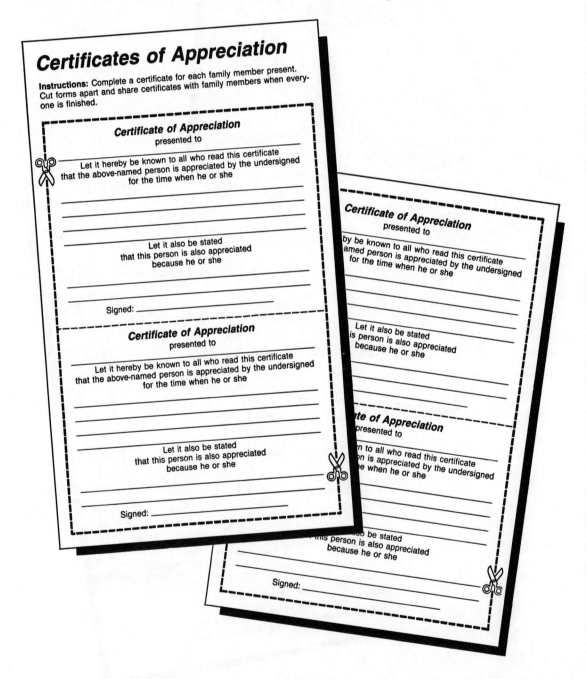

your child's sharing?

2. As young people, how did you feel about the fears, doubts and discouragements shared by your parents? Were you surprised? What did you want to do in response to your parent's sharing?

3. What ideas can you offer other families which might help them deal with the issues of fear, doubt and discouragement? (As people brainstorm their responses to this last question, record the ideas on newsprint.)

Pass out Bibles and ask each family unit to look at the bottom of the "Where Are You?" worksheet. Have each family read the Scriptural Insight passages and discuss how these apply to their own family members. Affirm the following observations: In Psalm 23, the psalmist knew God was stronger than fear. In Romans 8:37-39, Paul understood that we can never doubt God's love for us. In Philippians 4:10-13, Paul realized discouragement would never be stronger than hope in Christ.

Closing affirmation (5 minutes)—Have each person turn to the "Certificates of Appreciation." Point out that each page contains four certificates. Make sure each person has one certificate for each family member present. If someone needs more than four certificates, pass these out and redistribute the scissors. Allow time for individuals to complete their certificates and cut them apart. Use the last few minutes in family groups for individuals to share their certificates with each other.

Ask all families to gather in a large circle and hold hands. Ask individuals to share some of the discoveries that took place during this session. Recall Peter's life and how he was able to rise above his fears, doubts and discouragements. Close with prayer.

Explain the "Table Talk" worksheet to all participants. Encourage families to use this worksheet to explore this topic at home. Ask families to spend the next few minutes deciding when is the best time for their family members to meet during the coming week. Encourage them to write their scheduled time on their "Table Talk" worksheet and be responsible for keeping that time available. Remind everyone to bring his or her Participants Book back to the next session.

▰▰▰▰▰ Table Talk ▰▰▰▰▰

Instructions: "Table Talk" offers your family an opportunity to continue discussing the issue studied in class. Set aside 30 minutes for this family time.

But before you begin, remember one important thing: Practice listening as well as talking. Arguments, defensiveness, put-downs or shouting don't encourage conversation.

Now go ahead. Complete the following activity and make new discoveries about yourself and the other members of your family.

Our family "Table Talk" time this week will be _____
TIME
DAY

On the following form, write your name on the top line under My Family. Then list your current concern in each area. For example, if you doubt you can pass the science test, write "pass science test" under Doubt. If you are afraid of an upcoming job interview, write "interview" under Fear. Wait to write in the Help Wanted column until the directions tell you to do so.

My Family	Fear	Doubt	Discouragement	Help Wanted

After everyone has finished writing, share your concerns with the rest of your family. Take time to write others' concerns in your own book. Discuss ways you can help one another deal with the expressed concerns. Think about the kind of help you would like from your family.

Spend some time reflecting on Peter's life. Recall information learned from class discussions. Review the Scriptural Insights in the "Where Are You?" worksheet. Remind each other that Christ has the power to bring hope to your lives in the midst of fear, doubt and discouragement.

Tell family members what you would most like them to do to help you through the discouraging times you have listed. Listen to other family members' requests and write these in the last column under Help Wanted. Close with prayer.

"Let's Talk" Questions

Instructions: Use these questions to stimulate family discussion throughout the week. An ideal time is right after dinner.

1. As a junior high student, what are some of your fears, doubts and discouragements? As an adult, what were some of the fears, doubts and discouragements you faced in junior high? How are the struggles similar? How are they different?

2. How could you help a friend who is experiencing fear, doubt or discouragement?

3. Who were some other biblical characters who faced fear, doubt and discouragement? What can you learn from them?

4. What is one fear, doubt or discouragement you feel your family has in common? How can your family help one another deal with this problem?

5. Why might you or some of your family members not want to share personal experiences of fear, doubt or discouragement?

The Trap of Loneliness

Feelings of loneliness haunt both adults and adolescents. Adolescents struggle with body changes, unpredictable emotions and rejections that gang up to produce intense loneliness. Adults face the issues of work, family, personal value and midlife changes that create similar dark places of isolation.

This session helps parents and their children reflect on what causes loneliness and look at ways of getting through lonely times. Biblical passages lift up the good news that with God a person is never alone.

Objectives

During this session participants will:
- talk about times they have experienced loneliness.
- examine biblical characters who experienced lonely times.
- identify causes of loneliness.
- look at positive ways to help each other through times of feeling alone.

Biblical Foundation

Joseph struggles with the loneliness of his brothers' rejection: Genesis 37:1-28

Moses runs away to escape death: Exodus 2:11-15

Paul experiences the loneliness of being blind: Acts 9:1-9

Paul reassures people of God's continuing presence: Philippians 4:4-7

Background for Leader

Everyone needs time to be alone. Even Jesus withdrew

into the wilderness as a way to clarify his thoughts and feelings about what was happening in his life. Many adolescents and adults, however, wrestle with intense feelings of loneliness even while they are in a crowd. When self-esteem is low, people feel isolated. They magnify the feeling that no one cares until it paralyzes them. Consumed with feelings of inadequacy, lonely individuals become joyless creatures who view life through rainy skies.

In his book *All Grown Up & No Place to Go*, David Elkind presents a frank portrayal of the crises facing adolescents. The book pinpoints the inordinate amount of new stresses facing young people. Elkind says these stresses exist because of the excessive freedoms and increasing loss of security among young people. They become frustrated trying to cope with life issues in a school setting where attention to personal needs is almost impossible. The combination of these difficult experiences produces a powerful feeling of loneliness.

Today's pressures on adults can produce a similar effect. As adults face midlife changes and deal with their children's reactions to negative experiences, they are drained emotionally. Many adults mistakenly believe they should have all the answers and assume it's impossible for others to understand how they feel. They hesitate to share their lonely struggles with anyone, especially their children.

Listen carefully as group members share their thoughts and feelings during this study. Some may hint about the depth of their loneliness and reveal a need for support beyond the class period.

Preparation

Gather newsprint, markers, construction paper, Bibles, paper, pencils, masking tape, scissors, 3×5 cards, the tape or album *Between the Lines* by Janis Ian, and a tape or record player. If you can't find this album, use other contemporary music about loneliness and isolation.

Arrange chairs in a circle. On separate 3×5 cards write the names Joseph, Moses or Paul. Tape one card under the seat of each chair. Tape a card for each biblical character in three different locations around the room to indicate meeting places.

Tape three large sheets of newsprint to the wall.
Head one sheet "At Seventeen," another "I Feel Lonely
When . . ." and the other "The Bible Describes Loneliness
As . . ." Place a marker nearby.

Set up three long tables and cut a long sheet of newsprint for each mural in the Response section. Place construction paper, scissors, markers and masking tape on each
table.

Session

Opening (10 minutes)—Ask group members to seat
themselves in the circle. Pass out paper and pencils. Tell the
group: "I'm going to play a powerful song that talks about a
teenager's feelings of isolation. As I play 'At Seventeen,'
listen carefully and write words or phrases that describe
loneliness." After the song, ask the group to talk about what
they heard. Write responses on the newsprint titled "At
Seventeen." Then ask each person to turn to the person sitting next to him or her and discuss the following questions
as you read them aloud:

1. Why did the girl in the song feel so lonely?
2. What are some similar experiences in your own life?
3. When do you feel lonely?

After everyone has discussed these questions, ask for
responses to the last question and list these on the sheet of
newsprint titled "I Feel Lonely When . . ."

Theme presentation (15 minutes)—Tell the group to
turn in their Participants Book to the worksheet titled "Profiles of Loneliness." Tell the group: "You will be divided
into three small groups. Each group will be assigned a
biblical character from this worksheet. Read the scripture
passages assigned to your biblical character, answer the
questions and prepare a brief role play to introduce the
character's situation to the other groups. Involve both parents and young people in your role play."

Ask for questions. If there are none, point out the cards
that indicate the three meeting places. Tell group members
to check the 3×5 cards taped under their seats to see where
they should go. (If groups are overloaded with either par-

Profiles of Loneliness

Instructions: Read the scripture passage about the biblical character assigned to your group. Answer the questions that follow. Prepare a short role play to introduce this scripture passage to the other groups. Include both young people and parents in your presentation.

Joseph: Genesis 37:1-28
1. What happened to Joseph in this story?
2. What do you think Joseph felt when his brothers sold him into slavery?
3. In what ways do you think God was with Joseph during this time?
4. Have you ever felt "sold out"? Explain.

Moses: Exodus 2:11-15
1. What happened to Moses in this experience?
2. How do you think Moses felt when he ran away?
3. In what ways do you think God was still with Moses during this time?
4. Have you ever felt like a runaway? Explain.

Paul: Acts 9:1-9
1. What happened to Paul on the road to Damascus?
2. How do you think Paul felt after he was blinded?
3. In what ways do you think God was with Paul during this time?
4. Have you ever felt blind and alone? Explain.

20 Loneliness Lifters

Instructions: Complete each blank after careful consideration.

1. List three people with whom you enjoy spending time.

2. If you had time to read a good book, what would you read?

3. If you wanted to go somewhere to relax, where would you go?

4. Name someone who would enjoy a phone call from you.

5. Name someone who needs a letter from you.

6. What community organization could use your help?

7. What elderly person would enjoy your company?

8. What is your favorite type of exercise?

9. Who is going through some hard times and could use a big dose of your positive encouragement?

10. What project around your house needs your finishing touch?

11. What special activity does your family enjoy most?

12. What hobbies do you enjoy that you haven't done for a while?

13. In what area does your church need your help?

14. Name someone who could use a kind deed.

15. List three sections of the Bible you've always wondered about but never got around to reading. Read one of these.

16. Have you spent time talking with God lately?

17. Name someone you would enjoy taking to breakfast.

Name someone you would enjoy taking to lunch.

Name someone you would enjoy taking to dinner.

18. Who's your favorite shopping companion?

19. Invite someone to go with you to play your favorite sport.

20. Who would you enjoy taking to that movie you want to see?

Got those loneliness blahs? Put these 20 loneliness lifters into practice to lessen the intensity of your loneliness. Your actions can also bless others who are lonely.

ents or young people, make adjustments to mix the groups as evenly as possible. If each small group contains more than eight people, divide the groups in half and have two groups working on the same assignment.)

Exploration (10 minutes)—Gather the groups and have them present their role plays. Ask what they discovered about loneliness as they read their Bible stories. (Record responses on the newsprint titled "The Bible Describes Loneliness As . . .") Ask the following questions:

1. What are some things you have in common with these biblical characters?

2. How did loneliness affect the individual you studied?

3. How did these biblical characters handle their feelings so they could continue to live a full life?

Response (10 minutes)—Ask participants to re-form the three small groups they were in earlier. Give each group a large sheet of newsprint, several sheets of construction paper, markers and tape. Assign each group one of these three life situations: Friendships, Family or School/Work. Have each group create a collage of things that can cause individuals to experience loneliness in each situation. Tell groups to brainstorm and include as many ideas as possible. Remind group members they can use pictures or words to create their collages. Have individuals write or draw their ideas on separate sheets of construction paper, cut them into different sizes and shapes and tape them to the newsprint. After the groups are finished, have them tape their collages to the wall and explain their creations.

Closing affirmation (10 minutes)—Ask participants to turn in their books to the worksheet titled "20 Loneliness Lifters." Ask individuals to take time to respond to each question. After everyone is finished, go around the room and ask each individual to share one of his or her responses. Remind the group that these 20 items offer specific suggestions on ways to handle loneliness.

Read Philippians 4:4-7. Talk about Paul's view of how the good news helps us through times of loneliness. Talk about what it must have been like for Jesus to experience the cross—the ultimate experience of loneliness.

Affirm the importance of the "Table Talk" experience.

Encourage each family to decide now on a time to continue discussing this topic. Ask families to form their own circles and close by repeating to each family member, "God and I will support you in your loneliness."

Instructions: "Table Talk" offers your family an opportunity to continue discussing the issue studied in class. Set aside 30 minutes for this family time.

But before you begin, remember one important thing: Practice listening as well as talking. Arguments, defensiveness, put-downs or shouting don't encourage conversation.

Now go ahead. Complete the following activity and make new discoveries about yourself and the other members of your family.

> Our family "Table Talk" time this week will be _____
> TIME
> DAY

This week you talked about three biblical characters who experienced situations that produced loneliness. Reread the scripture passages on the "Profiles of Loneliness" worksheet. Continue reading the biblical stories beyond the point where you stopped in class.

1. What happened to each person?

2. What was the rest of his story?

3. How did God intervene in that person's life?

> Complete the following phrase: The times I feel most lonely in my family are

Be honest and open in your response. After everyone has finished, share what you have written. Then discuss the following questions together:

1. What causes each family member to feel lonely?

2. In what ways are you responsible for another family member's feelings of loneliness?

3. What can your family do to support each member when he or she feels lonely?

Complete the following statement:

I, _____, feel lonely when _____
My family can help me by:
1. _____
2. _____
3. _____
This will be our promise to one another.
Family members: _____

After you complete your form, pass it to each family member to read and sign. After everyone has signed your form, cut it out and tape it to the refrigerator. Seeing these forms each day will remind you of your promise to help one another ease those individual feelings of loneliness.

Let's Talk Questions

Instructions: Use these questions to stimulate family discussion throughout the week. An ideal time is right after dinner.

1. What was the loneliest experience you've ever had in school?

2. When did you feel most lonely this past week?

3. What did Jesus feel when he stood before the people and they wanted Barabbas instead? How would you have felt? (See Mark 15:7-15.)

4. How do you think God wants us to deal with our loneliness?

5. What are some positive ways we can help our friends through lonely times?

6. What's the best gift we can give someone when he or she feels lonely?

Faith Journeys: Fact or Fiction?

T he family and church provide important testing grounds for developing a personal faith. Family life provides important opportunities for faith exploration and formation. Individuals interact within the church to open and examine new faith frontiers. Within these environments, people discover that life develops a wholeness and meaning as their faith grows.

This session explores the realities of faith and stimulates thinking. What biblical characters provide models for faith formation? How can individuals find meaning through living and sharing their faith? How can a person know when he or she has faith? How can this faith be nurtured effectively? Questions like these form the focal point of this study.

Objectives
During this session participants will:
- talk about the biblical definition of faith.
- explore the faith of biblical characters.
- evaluate personal opinions about faith.
- make decisions about how to share their faith.

Biblical Foundation
Faith the size of a mustard seed can move mountains: Matthew 17:14-21

Even the disciples had weak moments in their faith: Mark 4:35-41

Individuals are justified by their faith: Romans 3:21-26

Faith comes when an individual hears and responds to

Christ's message: Romans 10:17

Faith is part of God's grace: Galatians 3:23-29

Faith is defined and documented in the action and statements of believers: Hebrews 11

Believers demonstrate an alive faith through action: James 2:14-17

Background for Leader

In his book *Spiritual Growth in Youth Ministry*, veteran youth minister J. David Stone points out that today's young people are searching for a viable faith. He presents personal experiences of being with adolescents while they struggle, reach out and stumble in their journey of faith. He says young people want to know how to build a spiritual life. They want to know how to apply Christian principles in an honest way. If the church can offer them an opportunity to experience spiritual growth, they will respond enthusiastically to Christ. Faith is important to young people.

James W. Fowler has spent many years researching and documenting how faith develops. In his book *Stages of Faith*, Fowler outlines six stages individuals may pass through as their faith develops. The first stage is usually associated with small children. It's a trusting and dependent faith based on imagination and feelings about what is seen and heard. The second stage is described as a "concrete faith" and usually evolves during a child's elementary years. During this time, imagination gives way to reality. The third stage usually occurs during adolescence. Individuals introduce their own thinking skills into their faith. The fourth stage begins to establish a personal faith after years of testing and observing others' values. The fifth and sixth stages symbolize a maturing faith, strong enough to be humble and confident enough to serve.

According to Fowler, most adolescents struggle within the third stage of faith development as they search for personal identity. Questions like "Who am I?" translate into faith issues like "What do I believe about God?" Interestingly, once individuals reach this stage of faith development, they often reside there for the rest of their adult lives.

Many biblical personalities' faith grew beyond the third stage and empowered them to greatness. This same kind of faith is available to each individual as he or she grows in response to God's grace.

Preparation

Gather pencils, markers, Bibles, masking tape, newsprint, two sheets each of red and blue construction paper, a record player and the album *Best of Bill Cosby*. This session will use the "Noah" selection from that album.

Arrange the chairs in a circle to begin the session. Tape a sheet of newsprint to the front wall and title it "Faith Is . . ."

Ask another adult to lead the parent group during the Exploration activity. Give him or her a copy of the "Faith Statements."

Arrange to use two rooms during this part of the session. Prepare two sets of three signs, one for each room. On the two sheets of red construction paper, write a large "False." On the two sheets of blue construction paper, write a large "True." On two 6-foot sheets of newsprint, write a large "Maybe." In each room, tape the "True" sign on one wall, tape the "False" sign on the opposite wall and tape the "Maybe" sign on the floor between the two walls. Place the signs at one end of the room so they won't be disturbed by other activities.

On separate sheets of newsprint, write each of the open-ended statements from the "My Faith" worksheet and hang them around the room.

Session

Opening (10 minutes)—As people arrive, have them sit in the circle. Play "Noah." After everyone has listened to this humorous account of Noah's talk with God, ask these questions:

1. What did God do to get Noah's attention?

2. What was Noah's initial reaction? Why do you think he reacted this way?

3. After Noah finally listened to God, how did he respond to God's request?

4. How did Noah react to his neighbors' taunts?

5. In what ways can your own response in faith bring you ridicule?

6. How would you define the word "faith"? (Write individuals' responses to this last question on the newsprint titled "Faith Is . . .")

Say: "Hebrews 11:1 tells us that faith is being sure of what we hope for and certain of what we don't see. Today we are going to explore the mystery of faith. First, we need a foundation for that mystery based on what the Bible says. Hebrews 11 will be our focal point."

Theme presentation (10 minutes)—Break into family groups. Be sure each family has pencils, Bibles and Participants Books. Tell families to turn to the worksheet titled "Faith Journeys." Ask them to work together to complete the biblical references.

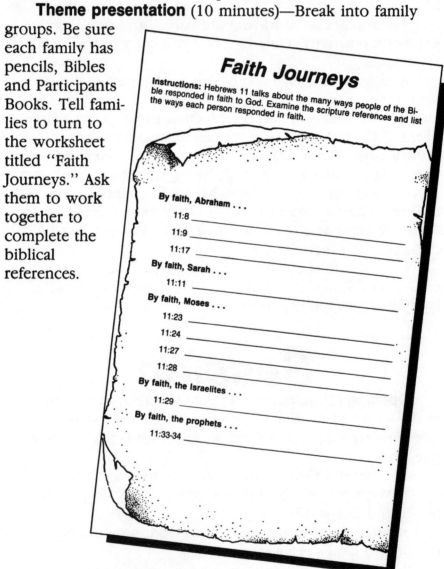

Faith Journeys

Instructions: Hebrews 11 talks about the many ways people of the Bible responded in faith to God. Examine the scripture references and list the ways each person responded in faith.

By faith, Abraham . . .

11:8 _____

11:9 _____

11:17 _____

By faith, Sarah . . .

11:11 _____

By faith, Moses . . .

11:23 _____

11:24 _____

11:27 _____

11:28 _____

By faith, the Israelites . . .

11:29 _____

By faith, the prophets . . .

11:33-34 _____

Exploration (15 minutes)—Separate the class into two groups, young people and adults. Tell them: "Many times we are unsure about what we believe. It's especially difficult to explain to others what we think about God or our faith. For the next few minutes we are going to examine our personal feelings about faith. Even though we do most things together, for this activity we will separate parents from young people so each person is free to express his or her opinion without the influence of the other."

Ask the adult leader to take the parents into another room while you lead the group of young people. The adult leader and you will each say: "I'm going to read 20 faith statements and ask for a response to each statement. You can answer in one of three ways. If you believe the statement is true, stand next to the blue sign labeled 'True.' If you believe the statement is false, stand next to the red sign labeled 'False.' If you are unsure, stand on the 'Maybe' sign in the middle.

Faith Statements

1. Faith comes automatically when you believe in God.
2. You must accept Jesus as Lord and Savior before you can have faith.
3. If you are a sincere Christian, you will never have doubts in your faith.
4. Faith can never be just a private thing between you and God. It must always be shared with others.
5. You have to wait until you are an adult before you can have real faith.
6. God alone decides who is going to have faith and who isn't.
7. Faith comes when you seek God in Christ and assume faithful obedience to him.
8. You can believe in God and still not have faith.
9. You can never know for sure if you have faith until it is tested.
10. If you do not share Christ with others, you do not have faith.
11. Prayer is an essential part of faith.
12. Wanting to care for others and be kind to them is a byproduct of faith.
13. Questioning God and his will indicates your faith is weak.
14. God's presence through the Holy Spirit energizes your faith.
15. If you don't read and study scripture, you can never have faith.
16. An adolescent can experience the same depth of faith as an adult.
17. Going to church is necessary for a growing faith.
18. Faith requires that you work at it to keep it.
19. It's easy to spot "false" Christians by their lack of faithful acts.
20. If you have faith, you are a better person than someone who doesn't have faith.

"These statements are meant to help you clarify your feelings about your faith, so listen carefully. I will read each statement twice. The first time, think about what I have read. The second time, move to your chosen position. Take a moment after each move to discuss your choice with the people who made the same choice."

Read each of the "Faith Statements" twice. Allow time for individuals to discuss their choices.

After reading the 20 statements, ask the group:

1. Why do you think it's difficult to tell others about your faith in God? Give specific reasons for your answer.

2. What did you learn about your faith from this activity?

Response (15 minutes)—Bring parents and young people back together. Ask everyone to turn to the "My Faith" worksheet and individually complete the responses.

Pass a marker to each person. Ask participants to move around the room to each open-ended statement and copy on the newsprint what they wrote in their Participants Book. After most people have finished, ask the group to return to the circle of chairs. As the group listens carefully, read some of the responses. Highlight similarities, differences and unique statements. Ask participants:

1. Which statements were hardest for you to complete? Why?

2. Why do you think faith is so difficult to understand?

Closing affirmation (5 minutes)—Ask one of your young people to read Romans 3:21-26. Talk about how this passage expresses Paul's belief that Christians are justified by faith. Reaffirm the idea that God's gift of grace means nothing unless the believer responds with faithful acceptance.

Ask a parent to read James 2:14-17. Ask the group: "Why is faith without action a dead faith?" After this closing discussion, remind each family to schedule their "Table Talk" session for the next week.

Ask everyone to form one large circle and hold hands. Remind the group: "We are all part of the larger family of God. When we have faith, we inherit the support of all Christians as part of our family." Close the session with a group hug.

My Faith

Instructions: Complete these open-ended statements:

I feel strongest in my faith when . . .

I feel weakest in my faith when . . .

The best thing I can do to help others grow in their faith is . . .

Three words that best describe my faith right now are . . .

A big question I have about my faith is . . .

The best gift of faith I can give my family is . . .

Table Talk

Instructions: "Table Talk" offers your family an opportunity to continue discussing the issue studied in class. Set aside 30 minutes for this family time.

But before you begin, remember one important thing: Practice listening as well as talking. Arguments, defensiveness, put-downs or shouting don't encourage conversation.

Now go ahead. Complete the following activity and make new discoveries about yourself and the other members of your family.

> Our family "Table Talk" time this week
> will be _____
> TIME
> DAY

Spend a few moments turning a paper cup into a symbol that says something about your faith. You can rip it, cut it, smash it, turn it upside down, fill it with water, etc. Share your creation with the rest of the family. What does it mean? Why did you create this particular symbol?

Go back to the "My Faith" worksheet. Give your response to "A big question I have about my faith is . . ." Talk about each person's response together.

1. What did you discover about the other members of your family?

2. How can you help each other find answers to a question like this?

Think of three things your family can do together to strengthen your faith:

1. _____
2. _____
3. _____

Discuss your ideas with the rest of your family. Based on each person's responses, work together to produce five definite steps your family will take to strengthen the faith of its members. List these steps under the heading "Family Faith Plan."

Family Faith Plan

_____
_____
_____
_____

Share your response from the "My Faith" worksheet to the statement "The best gift of faith I can give my family is . . ." Talk about what would happen if each person shared his or her special gift with the rest of the family. Make sharing this gift your personal goal for the rest of the week.

"Let's Talk" Questions

Instructions: Use these questions to stimulate family discussion throughout the week. An ideal time is right after dinner.

1. What one thing do you know about God of which you are absolutely certain?

2. If a stranger asked why you are a Christian, what would you say?

3. Think about people who lived during the last 100 years. What person had a strong faith and how did his or her life provide evidence of that faith?

4. If you could ask God one question and know it would be answered, what would that question be?

5. When have you been in a risky situation and put yourself in God's hands?

Impatience: Gift or Curse?

So many times society's "hurry up and get it done now" philosophy conspires against young people and their parents to produce impatience. Impatience robs individuals of the opportunity to enjoy life and its beauty and turns people into monsters who seem impossible to live with. It is no mistake that Paul lists patience as a fruit of the Spirit.

This session looks at patience as an important quality of life. It offers ways for individuals to develop or reclaim that quality within their relationships.

Objectives

During this session participants will:
- list characteristics of patient and impatient people.
- determine their personal patience levels.
- reflect on Jesus' views about patience.
- talk about ways to increase patience in their families.

Biblical Foundation

Jesus tells his followers not to worry: Matthew 6:25-34

Jesus illustrates his patience with the leper: Matthew 8:1-4

Jesus is amazed at the patience of the centurion: Matthew 8:5-13

Jesus demonstrates patience with his disciples: Matthew 8:23-27

Jesus is patient with Peter when he demonstrates a lack of faith: Matthew 14:28-31

Paul speaks of the importance of patience: Romans 8:25; 9:22; 12:12

Paul describes patience as a fruit of the Spirit: Galatians 5:22-23

This verse reminds new Christians to lay their minor concerns aside and concentrate on the important matters of faith: Hebrews 12:1

James instructs Christ's followers to be patient for the Lord's coming: James 5:7-8

Background for Leader

"If only people would have more patience with me." Everyone has heard or said that expression numerous times. Impatience steals the joy of the moment. The stalking presence of impatient attitudes and expectations is tough.

Patience is one of the most loving gifts to offer another human being, especially a family member. The biblical passages used in this session provide hints on how people can deal with impatience. Through Christ, individuals can become more gentle and accepting of themselves and others.

The junior high years test the patience levels of both parents and young people. Junior highers have trouble being patient with themselves, let alone other people. When parents help them recognize that impatience is a natural process of growing up, young people can work to sensitize themselves to the feelings of others. At the same time parents need to understand that increasing their own level of patience is essential if they are to help their adolescents grow in faith and love. Impatient attitudes only aggravate youthful discontent and confrontation.

Before leading this session, reflect on how you have dealt with impatience. By sharing some of your personal struggles with impatient attitudes, you will give participants permission to be more open about their impatience.

Preparation

Gather Bibles, pencils, newsprint, markers, crayons, masking tape and 3×5 cards.

Ask a parent to facilitate the parent group in the Exploration section while you work with the junior highers.

Tape a sheet of newsprint lengthwise across a wall and title it "Jesus' Ministry." Divide the newsprint into six columns with the following headings: Disciples, Sinners,

Crowds, Religious Figures, Outcasts and Healings.

On a separate sheet of newsprint, write this open-ended statement: "A Patient Person Is Someone Who Can . . ." Place a marker nearby.

Prepare the following scoring diagram for the "Patience Profiles" in the Exploration section:

My Patience Level

88-110 = I have no patience at all.

66-88 = I could use some more patience.

44-66 = My patience level is average.

22-44 = I am a very patient person.

Tape the diagram to the wall and cover it with another sheet of newsprint until it is needed.

Session

Opening (5 minutes)—Place two long sheets of newsprint on the floor. Have one parent lie on one sheet and one young person lie on the other sheet. Ask two other volunteers to use crayons to draw outlines of their bodies and title the sheets "Parent" and "Junior Higher." When the outlines are finished, draw a line down the middle of each page, splitting the image in half. Label the left side of each outline "Patience." Label the right side of each outline "Impatience." Hang these outlines at opposite ends of the room. Place a marker near each outline.

Ask parents to gather in front of the junior higher outline and young people to gather in front of the parent outline. Within each group assign one person to record the responses. Give these instructions: "List as many qualities, characteristics or actions as you can think of to describe a *patient* parent or young person. Then list as many qualities, characteristics or actions as you can think of to describe an *impatient* parent or young person. Record the responses on the appropriate side of the outlines."

After a few minutes place the outlines side by side and bring the two groups together to compare their responses. Tell both groups: "Look at the list of patient qualities listed by the other group. Which patient qualities do you feel are most important for a parent? Which patient qualities do you feel are most important for a junior higher?

"Look at the impatient qualities listed by the other group. Which impatient qualities do you think most parents are unaware of? Which impatient qualities do you think most junior highers are unaware of?

"Can you see yourself in any of these descriptions? Think about why your actions may seem patient or impatient to those around you. Decide on one impatient quality you would like to improve and concentrate on that quality throughout the rest of this session."

Theme presentation (10 minutes)—Share some personal experiences of how you have dealt with impatience in your own life. Include some of your mistakes along with your successes.

Ask the group to recall specific instances from Jesus' life when he demonstrated his patience. Write individual responses on the newsprint titled "Jesus' Ministry." Use some of the passages from the Biblical Foundation as examples if people have a hard time getting started.

After listing Jesus' patient qualities, ask the group to complete the open-ended statement written on the newsprint: "A Patient Person Is Someone Who Can . . ." List responses on the newsprint and then ask the group:

1. Why is having patience with yourself and others so difficult?

2. Does age affect your patience? Why or why not?

3. How can you gain patience?

4. Why do you think some people have more patience than others?

5. What does God have to do with patience?

Exploration (15 minutes)—Tell the class: "Each of you will have an opportunity to evaluate your individual patience level. Turn to the 'Patience Profile' worksheet. If you are a junior higher, use the junior high profile; if you are a parent, use the parent profile.

"The instructions for both worksheets are identical. Both profiles tell you to read each statement and rank that statement from 1 to 5 on how true it is for you. Circling a 1 means that statement is never true for you. Circling a 5 means that statement is always true. A 3 indicates that a statement is true at times, but not true at other times. Now

Patience Profile— *Junior Higher*

Instructions: This worksheet provides a way for you to determine your current patience level. Read each statement below. Rank yourself from 1 to 5 based on how true you feel that statement is for you (1 = never true; 5 = always true). Circle your response for each statement.

1. My teachers seem so unorganized.
2. My family expects too much from me.
3. I can't stand it when people waste my time.
4. I get bugged when things don't start on time.
5. I don't like it when a friend doesn't call me at the time he or she had promised.
6. Not having my favorite shirt clean ruins my day.
7. When people mess up my morning routine for getting ready for school, I get upset.
8. God seems so far away.
9. Sometimes I feel like I'll never amount to much.
10. Not being able to go out with my friends is like being in jail.
11. I sometimes feel like all this faith stuff is a waste of time.
12. Being told no by my parents really angers me.
13. I should always have first rights on TV programs.
14. Sunday morning church services are often boring to me.
15. Some people are such nerds.
16. I hate waiting in line.
17. Homework seems like a waste of time.
18. My parents never give me a straight answer about anything.
19. I don't like it when my friends aren't available to spend time with me.
20. Brothers and sisters are a pain in the neck.
21. Some people at school are real jerks.
22. Sometimes my friends do the dumbest things.

1 2 3 4 5
1 2 3 4 5
1 2 3 4 5
1 2 3 4 5
1 2 3 4 5

Patience Profile— *Parent*

Instructions: This worksheet provides a way for you to determine your current patience level. Read each statement below. Rank yourself from 1 to 5 based on how true you feel that statement is for you (1 = never true; 5 = always true). Circle your response for each statement.

1. Time is very important and should never be wasted. 1 2 3 4 5
2. A lot of people these days are extremely lazy. 1 2 3 4 5
3. People shouldn't make you spend time waiting for them. 1 2 3 4 5
4. I despise getting behind slow drivers. 1 2 3 4 5
5. I have high expectations for my family. 1 2 3 4 5
6. I notice that people often make dumb mistakes. 1 2 3 4 5
7. I get up most days feeling there is a hidden crisis waiting for me. 1 2 3 4 5
8. Waiting at train crossings drives me nuts. 1 2 3 4 5
9. It's never okay for family members to make plans for me without asking me first. 1 2 3 4 5
10. I have more work to do than time to do it. 1 2 3 4 5
11. A person should always do a job right the first time. 1 2 3 4 5
12. Rainy Saturdays destroy my weekends. 1 2 3 4 5
13. I usually don't finish many of the books I start. 1 2 3 4 5
14. I have high expectations for myself. 1 2 3 4 5
15. Being gentle with people is a sign of weakness. 1 2 3 4 5
16. Some people never catch on no matter how many times you explain something to them. 1 2 3 4 5
17. When God handed out talent, I must have been left out. 1 2 3 4 5
18. Spiritual nurturing is not important to me. 1 2 3 4 5
19. Church services should never go beyond one hour. 1 2 3 4 5
20. Junior highers seem to enjoy driving you crazy. 1 2 3 4 5
21. I can't stand waiting in line at checkout counters. 1 2 3 4 5
22. Drive-up windows are the ultimate frustration. 1 2 3 4 5

spend a few minutes circling your responses."

After individuals finish circling their responses, have them total the points. Uncover the scoring diagram so they can see how patient they really are. Ask the appointed adult leader to meet with the parents at the back of the room while you meet with the kids at the front of the room. Discuss items such as discoveries about patience levels, reasons participants scored as they did, which statements were circled as a 5 or a 1, etc.

Response (20 minutes)—Spend the rest of this session reflecting on what causes impatient times between parents and junior highers. Keep the class separated into groups at opposite ends of the room. Give each group a stack of 3×5 cards. Allow five minutes for parents to think of as many responses as they can to the statement, "My junior higher tries my patience when . . ." Allow the same amount of time for kids to complete the statement, "My parents try my patience when . . ." Instruct group members to write one response on each 3×5 card. Encourage participants to be as specific as possible without using names or revealing confidential issues in their families.

At the end of the five minutes, take up the cards from each group. Ask parents and young people to form one large circle. Tell everyone you are going to alternate reading each group's statements. As you read a statement from one group, ask someone from the other group to share his or her point of view. For example, you could read, "My junior higher tries my patience when he stays out too late on a school night." Then allow junior highers time to respond to that statement. Next read a statement written by a junior higher. Let the parents respond.

Often parents and young people aren't aware of personal behaviors that provoke impatience in others. This process may reveal some of those behaviors and cause participants to look critically at themselves. Insist on positive feedback aimed at promoting understanding. Encourage participants to think of ways to eliminate or deal with these stresses on one another. Remind both groups to use this time for constructive growth, not destructive confrontation.

Closing affirmation (5 minutes)—As you bring this session to a close, affirm the sharing that has taken place. Talk about the efforts of both parents and young people to open new doors of understanding.

Ask a young person to read Matthew 6:25-34. Challenge participants to ask for God's help in building patience in their lives. Remind individuals that as they accept and share God's love, their patience toward others will grow.

Remind families to schedule their "Table Talk" time for this week. Ask groups of two or three families to form a circle. Have them offer sentence prayers of thanks for the patience they discovered in their family and in themselves.

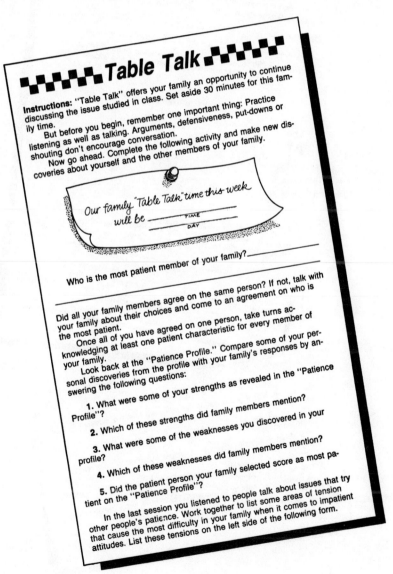

◢◣◢◣◢◣Table Talk◢◣◢◣◢◣

Instructions: "Table Talk" offers your family an opportunity to continue discussing the issue studied in class. Set aside 30 minutes for this family time.

But before you begin, remember one important thing: Practice listening as well as talking. Arguments, defensiveness, put-downs or shouting don't encourage conversation.

Now go ahead. Complete the following activity and make new discoveries about yourself and the other members of your family.

Our family "Table Talk" time this week will be _____ TIME _____ DAY

Who is the most patient member of your family?_____

_____

Did all your family members agree on the same person? If not, talk with your family about their choices and come to an agreement on who is the most patient.

Once all of you have agreed on one person, take turns acknowledging at least one patient characteristic for every member of your family.

Look back at the "Patience Profile." Compare some of your personal discoveries from the profile with your family's responses by answering the following questions:

1. What were some of your strengths as revealed in the "Patience Profile"?

2. Which of these strengths did family members mention?

3. What were some of the weaknesses you discovered in your profile?

4. Which of these weaknesses did family members mention?

5. Did the patient person your family selected score as most patient on the "Patience Profile"?

In the last session you listened to people talk about issues that try other people's patience. Work together to list some areas of tension that cause the most difficulty in your family when it comes to impatient attitudes. List these tensions on the left side of the following form.

Brainstorm ways your family can deal more effectively with these areas of tension. Record these ideas on the right side of the following form. Circle the areas of tension for which you feel responsible.

Areas of Tension	How to Deal With These Tensions

Complete the following statement: The one thing I do that tries others' patience most is _____.

Work together as a family to list five positive steps all of you will take to make your family atmosphere more patient and understanding for one another.

Five Positive Steps

Examine the list of positive steps toward patience your family has just created. How can you become a positive influence in this process? Complete the patience contract below and share its content with family members.

Patience Contract

I, _____, agree to become a more patient influence in my family by doing the following: _____.

I will begin working on that step immediately.

Signed: _____

"Let's Talk" Questions

Instructions: Use these questions to stimulate family discussion throughout the week. An ideal time is right after dinner.

1. Outside your family, what do people do to you that tries your patience the most?

2. What is something you wish people would do to be more patient with you?

3. Outside your family, what experiences have you had this week that wrecked your patience?

4. What could nations of the world do to have more patience with each other?

5. How do you think God wants you to handle your impatience?

Anger: Good News and Bad News

S ome people have been taught that anger is an unchristian emotion. Many have heard that getting angry with someone is a sin. What kind of attitude should Christians have toward anger?

Anger is an emotion packed with explosive force. How should people deal with their anger? How did Jesus handle his anger? Is it ever okay to be angry with ourselves or with other people? What is the most loving Christian response to anger?

All parents and young people face moments of anger. This session will help individuals share their viewpoints and understand effective ways for families to deal with this emotion.

Objectives

During this session participants will:
- talk about experiences that have made them angry.
- look at the results of angry actions that have taken place within our society.
- reflect on a biblical perspective about anger.
- examine healthy and unhealthy ways to express anger.

Biblical Foundation

Moses confronts the golden calf worshipers: Exodus 32:7-29

Nathan confronts King David: 2 Samuel 12:1-7a

Jesus reminds the people not to be angry with their brothers: Matthew 5:21-24

Jesus drives the money changers from the temple: Matthew 21:12-13

Jesus says exactly what he thinks about the Pharisees: Matthew 23:1-36

Jesus becomes angry because people cannot see the greater good: Mark 3:1-6

Speak truthfully; don't let the sun go down on your anger: Ephesians 4:25-27, 29

Background for Leader

Angry confrontations can rip family relationships. Little disagreements and misunderstandings sometimes erupt into major arguments. People raise their voices, muscles tighten, nerves tense, and suddenly angry shouts and indignant remarks pollute the atmosphere. Anger can get ugly at times, and people accomplish nothing when they merely spew anger's harmful poison.

How can parents and young people equip themselves to deal with anger more effectively? Individuals can learn to use communication styles that allow people to share their angry feelings in healthy, Christian ways.

The Bible treats anger as a natural part of life. It provides numerous examples of how different people handled this emotion in various situations. The Bible also reassures individuals that to feel anger is not a sin; the way people deal with anger and how they express hostile feelings determine whether anger is a sin.

Anger acts as a destructive roadblock in any relationship. Helping families agree how to handle anger is a major step forward in tearing down the walls that block communication. When parents and their children recognize the healthy and unhealthy ways of sharing anger, they are freed to help each other enjoy healthier and happier Christian lifestyles.

Preparation

Gather newsprint, tape, markers, Bibles, pencils, newspapers, news magazines, scissors, construction paper and three small tables.

Tape three long sheets of newsprint on the walls to use as murals. Place a table below each sheet of newsprint. Divide a generous supply of newspapers and news magazines among the three tables. In addition, place on each table construction paper, scissors, markers and tape. Prepare three copies of the following set of directions and tape these to each table:

Mural Instuctions

   1. Look through the newspapers and magazines for pictures or words that illustrate how anger is expressed in our world today.
   2. Cut out these illustrations and tape them to the newsprint at this location.
   3. On construction paper, write or draw expressions of anger not found in the resources provided. Tape these expressions to the newsprint.

Tape a sheet of newsprint to the wall and title it "Incidents of Anger."

Copy the following diagram on a large sheet of newsprint and tape it to the front wall.

How Do I Deal With My Anger?

Negative, Unchristian Ways to Deal With Anger

When I am angry with others	When others are angry with me
1.	1.
2.	2.
3.	3.
4.	4.
5.	5.

Positive, Christian Ways to Deal With Anger

When I am angry with others	When others are angry with me
1.	1.
2.	2.
3.	3.
4.	4.
5.	5.

Session

Opening (10 minutes)—As people arrive, ask them to go to one of the tables and read the instructions. Encourage families to go to the same table and work together. When the murals are finished, go around the room and reflect on the horrible realities presented. Ask: "What do these illustrations tell you about the level of anger in our world today? What do they tell you about the ways people deal with their anger? How do you feel about what you have just seen?"

Theme presentation (15 minutes)—Tell the group: "Anger has been with us a long time. Beginning with the story of Cain and Abel, the Bible describes relationships altered by anger. Everyone has experienced this intense emotion at one time or another; it is part of human nature. What you do about your anger, how you express it and whether you use this emotion to build or destroy relationships determine whether your response is Christian or sinful. Today you are going to explore several angry situations in the Bible."

Divide the class into four smaller groups by having parents and kids number off by fours. Have all the ones form a group, all the twos, etc. Distribute Bibles and assign each small group one of the following incidents:

Moses confronts the golden calf worshipers: Exodus 32:7-29

Nathan confronts King David: 2 Samuel 12:1-7a

Jesus says exactly what he thinks about the Pharisees: Matthew 23:1-36

Jesus becomes angry because people cannot see the greater good: Mark 3:1-6

Tell the groups they have five minutes to read their assigned scripture passages and prepare a short role play of their incidents. Remind groups they don't have to use every verse, just present a dramatic replay of what happened. Ask groups to include any kind of angry emotions the Bible characters might have experienced.

After groups have prepared their role plays, have them gather in the front of the room. Tell everyone to turn to the worksheet titled "Incidents of Anger." Explain that as each

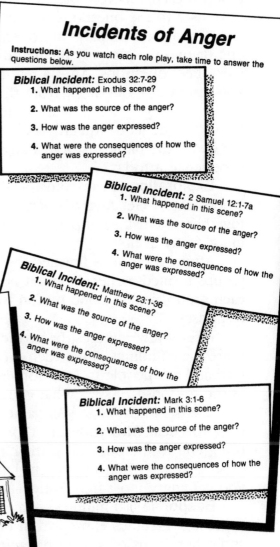

Incidents of Anger

Instructions: As you watch each role play, take time to answer the questions below.

Biblical Incident: Exodus 32:7-29
1. What happened in this scene?

2. What was the source of the anger?

3. How was the anger expressed?

4. What were the consequences of how the anger was expressed?

Biblical Incident: 2 Samuel 12:1-7a
1. What happened in this scene?

2. What was the source of the anger?

3. How was the anger expressed?

4. What were the consequences of how the anger was expressed?

Biblical Incident: Matthew 23:1-36
1. What happened in this scene?

2. What was the source of the anger?

3. How was the anger expressed?

4. What were the consequences of how the anger was expressed?

Biblical Incident: Mark 3:1-6
1. What happened in this scene?

2. What was the source of the anger?

3. How was the anger expressed?

4. What were the consequences of how the anger was expressed?

I Get ANGRY When . . .

Instructions: What makes you really angry? Examine the four open-ended statements and list some things that make you angry in each area of your life.

I get angry with my friends when . . .

I get angry at school when . . .

I get angry at home when . . .

I get angry with myself when . . .

group presents its role play, observers should write their responses to the questions on the worksheet.

When the role plays are over, ask individuals to turn to one or two people near them and discuss responses to the worksheet questions. After a few minutes ask, "What did you discover about anger from these scenes?" Summarize responses as you write them on the sheet of newsprint titled "Incidents of Anger." Ask, "What is similar or different about the biblical story of anger and the way we experience it today?"

Exploration (15 minutes)—Ask the class to turn to the worksheet "I Get Angry When . . ." Read the instructions together, and ask each person to respond to the statements individually at first.

After everyone is finished, break into the four small groups formed earlier. Pass out newsprint and a marker to each group, and ask one person to record everyone's responses.

After a few minutes, bring the groups together to briefly share their findings. Tape each group's newsprint to the wall and ask people to look for similarities and differences in the responses. Ask: "What issues seem to recur? How can you use the knowledge you gained from this experience to help you deal with your anger? What one thing tends to bring you to the point of getting angry? How do you usually express anger when you reach that point? With whom do you get angry most frequently—family or friends? Why?"

Response (10 minutes)—Say: "You have seen how anger is sometimes expressed in our society—war, murder and other forms of violent behavior. You have examined situations in the Bible where anger was expressed. You have shared things about personal relationships that anger you at times.

"Now comes the tough part. What is the most loving, Christian way you can deal with those angry feelings? Look at the diagram taped to the front wall. Let's brainstorm some ideas for each part of the diagram on 'How Do I Deal With My Anger?' " As people give their ideas, write them in the appropriate section of the diagram.

Closing affirmation (5 minutes)—Break the group into family units. Ask a parent to read Ephesians 4:25-27, 29. Ask

◤◥◤◥◤◥ Table Talk ◤◥◤◥◤◥

Instructions: "Table Talk" offers your family an opportunity to continue discussing the issue studied in class. Set aside 30 minutes for this family time.

But before you begin, remember one important thing: Practice listening as well as talking. Arguments, defensiveness, put-downs or shouting don't encourage conversation.

Now go ahead. Complete the following activity and make new discoveries about yourself and the other members of your family.

Our family "Table Talk" time this week will be _____
TIME
_____
DAY

On the following form, list each family member in the center column. Then complete the directions on either side of the column.

Family Members

List one thing about each person that makes you angry.	Name	List one thing you do to each person that makes him or her angry.

Talk about your list with the rest of the family. After examining others' lists, ask yourself the following questions:

1. Which items do you agree with? _____ Why? _____

2. Which items do you disagree with? _____ Why? _____

3. What behavior can you change to help you deal with the anger in your family in a more Christian way? _____

4. What have been some destructive ways in which your family has dealt with anger? _____ Who was hurt? _____

5. What have been some positive ways in which your family has dealt with anger? _____

Family Action Plan

Work with your family to set up an action plan for dealing with anger. Complete this statement:

When people in my family are angry, I will:

1.
2.
3.
4.
5.

a young person to read Matthew 5:21-24. Encourage everyone to use what Paul and Jesus say about dealing with anger. Remind participants that anger expressed with love and a positive Christian attitude builds relationships rather than wrecks them.

Ask family members to thank the person on their right for one example of his or her openness during this session. After a few minutes ask families to join hands and each individual to pray for the person on his or her left. Close this session by encouraging families to continue their discussions at home. Remind them to schedule a time for this week's "Table Talk."

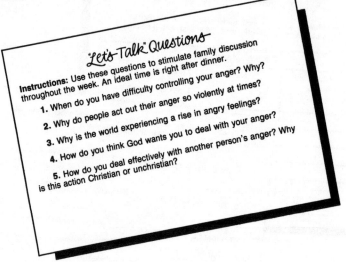

"Let's Talk" Questions

Instructions: Use these questions to stimulate family discussion throughout the week. An ideal time is right after dinner.

1. When do you have difficulty controlling your anger? Why?

2. Why do people act out their anger so violently at times?

3. Why is the world experiencing a rise in angry feelings?

4. How do you think God wants you to deal with your anger?

5. How do you deal effectively with another person's anger? Why is this action Christian or unchristian?

Burned at the Stake: Facing or Creating Persecution

Persecution brings pain. Being wronged by others, particularly friends or family, cuts deep. This kind of pain comes in many forms—being laughed at, condemned, passed over, left out and so on. The junior high years are full of persecution, both real and imagined, as young people experience a level of sensitivity that is heightened to unrealistic proportions. Parents also experience the burning sting of persecution. When they are passed over for a promotion, phased out of a job, caught by a betrayed confidence, manipulated, laughed at or ignored, they experience the same pain as their children.

This session testifies to the fact that Christians can survive life's painful moments of ridicule and rejection. By recognizing the power of God's love and realizing this love is meant for everyone, individuals can overcome persecution, no matter how painful it may be.

Objectives

During this session participants will:
- identify ways they feel persecuted.
- identify ways they sometimes persecute others.
- read about incidents of persecution in the Bible.
- discover God's promises for helping them through times of persecution.

Biblical Foundation

Jacob cheats Esau: Genesis 27:18-35
Saul hates David: 1 Samuel 18:6-11
Elijah is hunted by Jezebel: 1 Kings 19:1-4
The disciples are put on trial: Matthew 10:16-20
John is used as a pawn and beheaded: Matthew 14:1-10
A woman is put down by the disciples: Matthew 26:6-9
Jesus is laughed at: Mark 5:35-43
Children are rejected: Mark 10:13-16
Jesus is denied by Peter: Luke 22:54-57
Jesus is passed over for Barabbas: Luke 23:8-25
Paul is beaten, whipped and stoned: 2 Corinthians 11:24-25

Background for Leader

The Bible contains vivid examples of people who faced horrible persecution. These stories weave the tapestry of salvation in biblical history. Every form of persecution that people face today has already been faced by other individuals in the past. God was with his people then and continues to be with them today.

Persecution takes a heavy toll on junior highers. They are facing not only physical changes, but also intense emotional needs for personal acceptance. Any form of rejection, whether real or perceived, becomes painful persecution in their minds. At this age young people can feel devastated and are sure life will always stay the same. Young people need to know how to use the experiences of persecution as opportunities for personal growth.

Parenting a junior higher is also painful. It requires making tough, unpopular decisions and disciplining adolescents who see these efforts as deliberate attempts to persecute them. Helping parents and their children balance the motives behind decisions and discipline is important.

The Bible can become a resource to affirm God's presence during times of persecution. As participants examine the perseverance displayed by their biblical ancestors, they can learn to stand firm in the face of adversity. This position doesn't mean individuals will never face persecution; it means simply that people can learn to conquer their persecution by growing from it and even helping others in the midst of their pain.

Preparation

Gather newsprint, red and black markers, gray and brown construction paper, scissors, masking tape, pencils, Bibles, a long table and a trash basket. Collect in a bowl one small rock for each person.

On a long sheet of newsprint, draw an outline of a person and write the heading "I Feel Persecuted When . . ." Tape this outline to the wall and place a red marker nearby. Cut stone shapes from the gray and brown construction paper and place these on the long table along with black markers and masking tape. Tape sample stones like the following to the outline:

"I feel persecuted when my big sister gets good grades and calls me stupid."

"I feel persecuted when everyone goes out after supper and leaves me with all the dishes."

Ask an adult volunteer to stay at the table to clarify directions as people arrive.

Tape three more sheets of newsprint to the front wall and one to the opposite wall. Title the first sheet "Words That Hurt Me." On the second sheet, prepare a large duplicate of "The Pain of Persecution" worksheet in the Participants Book. Title the two remaining sheets "Stones I Throw" and draw a vertical line down the center of each sheet from top to bottom. Place black markers nearby.

Session

Opening (10 minutes)—As people arrive, ask them to move to the table in the center of the room. Have your helper tell them what to do. Ask participants to write on the construction paper stones as many responses as they can think of to the statement "I feel persecuted when . . ." Have them tape these anywhere on the body outline taped to the front wall. Participants may want to consult the sample stones taped to the outline for ideas.

After five minutes, ask the group members to form a semicircle with their chairs in front of the outline. Ask each person to read one of the paper rocks on the outline, beginning with the phrase "I feel persecuted when . . ." Mark each rock with the red marker as it is read. Ask the group:

1. What similar kinds of persecutions do you see?
2. What persecutions seem aimed only at parents?
3. What persecutions seem aimed only at kids?

Theme presentation (5 minutes)—Pass the bowl of small rocks. Ask everyone to take a rock and keep it with them throughout the rest of this session. As the bowl passes, ask people to focus on the rock they are holding. Ask them to study it for a moment and think about its characteristics. When everyone has a rock, ask the group to list the characteristics of a rock such as hard, jagged, sharp and so on. Then ask, "What do you think it would feel like to get hit by a rock?"

Ask one young person and one parent to volunteer to stand at the front of the room. After they are in position, tell the rest of the group, "Stand, face the front and raise your rocks as if you were going to stone these two people." (Pause for a few seconds.)

Ask the group: "If I had said, 'Throw your rocks as hard as you can on the count of three,' how would you have felt? Would you have thrown your rocks?" After participants respond, ask, "What would have happened to these two people if all of you had thrown your rocks?"

Ask the two volunteers, "How did you feel when you saw everyone ready to throw their rocks?" After the two volunteers respond, tell the group: "Every time we feel persecuted, it's just like getting hit with a rock. It hurts. It stings. It cuts deep. It leaves scars. Look at the 'I Feel Persecuted When . . .' outline. On every rock we see red. This red represents our blood, our pain of persecution.

"All of us have heard the old saying 'Sticks and stones may break my bones, but words will never hurt me.' What's wrong with that saying?"

When someone answers that words are just another form of persecution, say: "Words do hurt, don't they? Sometimes stinging words are more painful than sharp rocks. List some words or phrases that hurt when people throw them at you." Ask someone to record the different responses on the newsprint titled "Words That Hurt Me."

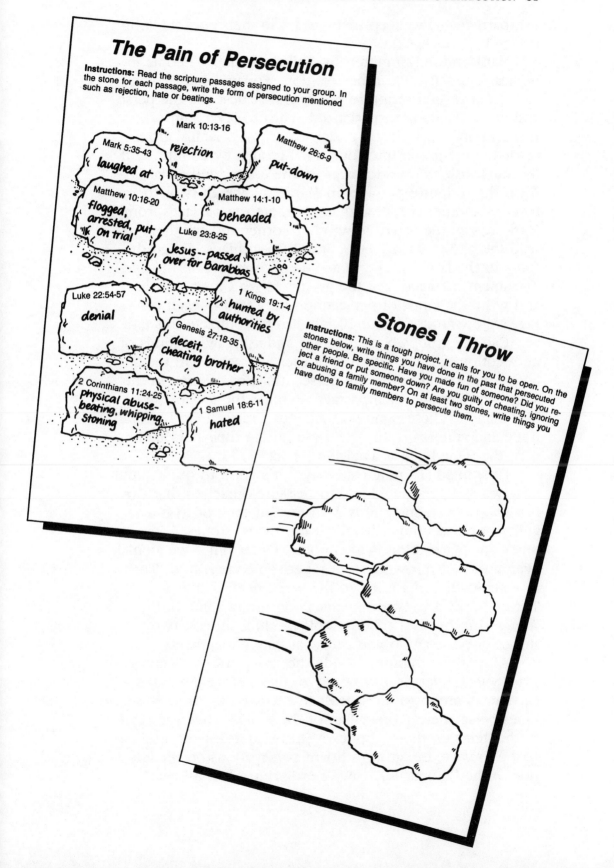

The Pain of Persecution

Instructions: Read the scripture passages assigned to your group. In the stone for each passage, write the form of persecution mentioned such as rejection, hate or beatings.

Mark 10:13-16
rejection

Mark 5:35-43
laughed at

Matthew 26:6-9
put-down

Matthew 10:16-20
flogged, arrested, put on trial

Matthew 14:1-10
beheaded

Luke 23:8-25
Jesus -- passed over for Barabbas

Luke 22:54-57
denial

1 Kings 19:1-4
hunted by authorities

Genesis 27:18-35
deceit, cheating brother

2 Corinthians 11:24-25
physical abuse- beating, whipping, stoning

1 Samuel 18:6-11
hated

Stones I Throw

Instructions: This is a tough project. It calls for you to be open. On the stones below, write things you have done in the past that persecuted other people. Be specific. Have you made fun of someone? Did you reject a friend or put someone down? Are you guilty of cheating, ignoring or abusing a family member? On at least two stones, write things you have done to family members to persecute them.

Ask participants to keep their stones in their pockets until the end of the session.

Exploration (20 minutes)—Tell the group: "People in biblical times also faced persecution. Today we are going to look at several scripture passages that describe the persecution these people experienced. Turn to 'The Pain of Persecution' worksheet." Assign passages to family groups, or divide the group into four small groups by counting off by fours. Ask all ones to meet in one corner and assign them the scripture passages in Matthew. Ask all twos to meet in another corner and assign them the passages from Mark. Assign the threes to another corner and ask them to read the passages from Luke and 2 Corinthians. Assign the fours to the last corner and ask them to report on the Old Testament passages. Tell the groups to read their passages and write the kinds of persecution they find in each passage. Allow groups about 10 minutes to complete this task.

Call the groups back together and ask, "What kinds of persecution did you discover in each passage?" On the enlarged worksheet, write the persecutions mentioned in the stone representing each passage. Remind the group: "We face many of these same persecutions today. If God offered hope and comfort to these people during their persecution, then the same hope is available for us."

Response (15 minutes)—Say: "It's good to think about how we feel persecuted and to reassure ourselves that God has always been and still is with us. But each of us is also guilty of persecuting others; we too throw stones. Sometimes our persecution is intentional. Other times we aren't even aware of throwing stones, yet someone is hurt. Turn in your Participants Book to the worksheet 'Stones I Throw.' Spend a few moments alone listing some of the stones you throw at other people. Include at least two stones of persecution you throw at family members."

After a few minutes, divide the group into kids and parents. Select a person from each group to serve as scribe. Ask each small group to list at least five to 10 ways they sometimes persecute the other half of the group. They can refer to the items on their "Stones I Throw" worksheet. Ask the scribe to write the group's list of persecutions on the left side of the "Stones I Throw" newsprint. Then ask each group, "What can you do to stop these kinds of persecutions in your family?" Have the scribe list these responses on the right side of the newsprint.

Bring the groups back together. Hang the two lists side by side and compare the findings. Ask the kids: "Can you think of any persecutions not listed on the parents' sheet? Can you think of any additional solutions to the persecutions listed here?" Ask the parents: "Can you think of any persecutions not listed on the kids' sheet? Can you think of any additional solutions to the persecutions listed here?" Talk about the ways parents and junior highers persecute one another.

Closing affirmation (5 minutes)—Ask the group members to form a circle and retrieve their rocks from their pockets. Tell the group: "Each of us is guilty of hurting others. As a first step toward healing the hurts within our families, think about one stone or persecution you would like to eliminate from your life. As the trash basket passes around the room, throw your rock away and pray silently about the persecution you've chosen to eliminate. Let this action symbolize your willingness to work on not being a source of persecution within your family."

Pass the trash basket around the room. After everyone has thrown his or her rock into the basket have a parent read 2 Corinthians 11:24-25. Remind the group: "Even though Paul faced all kinds of persecution, he continued to live his life with enthusiasm. If Paul could continue while enduring this kind of physical and emotional abuse, surely God has equipped us with enough faith to live through our own tough times of persecution. If God loved us enough to allow his only Son to be nailed to a cross, his love will support us through any persecution we may encounter."

Remind families to schedule their "Table Talk" time for the coming week. Close the session by asking family groups to hold hands. Say: "Affirm the family member on your right. Thank him or her for something positive he or she does to eliminate persecution in your family. Perhaps your brother teases family members to keep everyone in a good mood or maybe your dad is great at listening to both sides of an issue. Pray for God's help as you deal with persecution, both the kind you receive and the kind you generate."

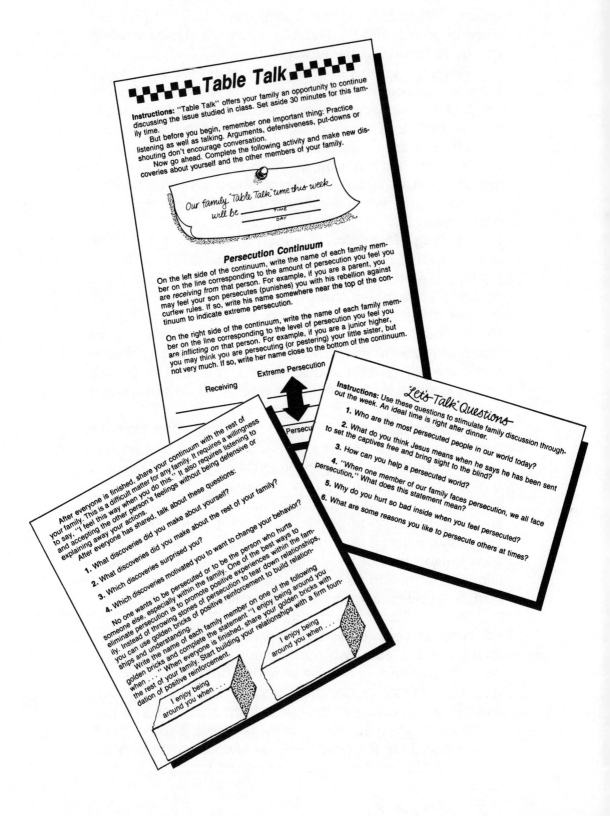

⌐⌐⌐⌐Table Talk⌐⌐⌐⌐

Instructions: "Table Talk" offers your family an opportunity to continue discussing the issue studied in class. Set aside 30 minutes for this family time.

But before you begin, remember one important thing: Practice listening as well as talking. Arguments, defensiveness, put-downs or shouting don't encourage conversation.

Now go ahead. Complete the following activity and make new discoveries about yourself and the other members of your family.

Our family "Table Talk" time this week will be _____
TIME
DAY

Persecution Continuum

On the left side of the continuum, write the name of each family member on the line corresponding to the amount of persecution you feel you are *receiving* from that person. For example, if you are a parent, you may feel your son persecutes (punishes) you with his rebellion against curfew rules. If so, write his name somewhere near the top of the continuum to indicate extreme persecution.

On the right side of the continuum, write the name of each family member on the line corresponding to the level of persecution you feel you are *inflicting* on that person. For example, if you are a junior higher, you may think you are persecuting (or pestering) your little sister, but not very much. If so, write her name close to the bottom of the continuum.

Extreme Persecution

Receiving

Persec[ut]

"Let's Talk" Questions

Instructions: Use these questions to stimulate family discussion throughout the week. An ideal time is right after dinner.

1. Who are the most persecuted people in our world today?
2. What do you think Jesus means when he says he has been sent to set the captives free and bring sight to the blind?
3. How can you help a persecuted world?
4. "When one member of our family faces persecution, we all face persecution." What does this statement mean?
5. Why do you hurt so bad inside when you feel persecuted?
6. What are some reasons you like to persecute others at times?

After everyone is finished, share your continuum with the rest of your family. This is a difficult matter for any family. It requires a willingness to say, "I feel this way when you do this." It also requires listening to and accepting the other person's feelings without being defensive or explaining away your actions.

After everyone has shared, talk about these questions:

1. What discoveries did you make about yourself?
2. What discoveries did you make about the rest of your family?
3. Which discoveries surprised you?
4. Which discoveries motivated you to want to change your behavior?

No one wants to be persecuted or to be the person who hurts someone else, especially within the family. One of the best ways to eliminate persecution is to promote positive experiences within the family. Instead of throwing golden bricks of persecution to tear down relationships, you can use golden bricks of positive reinforcement to build relationships and understanding.

Write the name of each family member on one of the following golden bricks and complete the statement "I enjoy being around you when . . ." When everyone is finished, share your golden bricks with the rest of your family. Start building your relationships with a firm foundation of positive reinforcement.

I enjoy being around you when . . .

I enjoy being around you when . . .

How Big the Apple? How Great the Temptation?

*T*emptation is a menace to family life. Junior highers and their parents are tempted in many daily struggles at home, school or work. How can families stand up to temptation? How can faith help?

This session looks at the seductive nature of temptation It helps young people and their parents work together to loosen the grip of this tantalizing force on their lives.

Objectives

During this session participants will:
- identify some of the temptations they face.
- reflect on biblical characters who faced temptation.
- affirm a Christian strategy for dealing with temptation.

Biblical Foundation

Temptation themes:
Hatred and jealousy: Genesis 4:3-8
Lying: Genesis 12:10-19
Cheating and stealing: Genesis 27:15-40
Complaining: Exodus 16:2-3
Sexual gratification: 2 Samuel 11:1-26
Judging: Matthew 7:1-5
Riches: Matthew 19:16-22
Hypocrisy: Matthew 23:1-7
Laziness: Matthew 25:14-30

Power: Mark 10:35-37
Doubt: John 20:24-25
Vengeance: Romans 12:19-21
Adam and Eve's struggle with temptation: Genesis 2:15-22, 25; 3:1-13
Paul struggles with sin: Romans 7:18-25
Paul advises Christ's followers to put on the armor of God: Ephesians 6:13-18a

Background for Leader

The Bible supplies a continuing saga of human beings lured by temptation. People today also face daily temptations that urge them to compromise and give in to that which is easier or more convenient. The mind cannot escape the tendency to go against God's plan. Young people and parents alike face tough decisions that tempt them to turn away from God and chart their own way. Age offers little protection from temptation.

The biblical narrative is frank; it never tries to de-emphasize the power of temptation. It describes the continuous struggle of human beings to say no, from Adam and Eve to King David and so on. Even Jesus experienced temptation, yet he did not give in (Matthew 4:1-11). He became the model for helping people stand firm in the midst of life's sinful enticements.

Many kinds of temptation confront parents and young people. It's important to understand the universal way temptation enters a person's life. First doubt creeps into an individual's mind. Then it plants itself, and the power of right within the heart gives way to temptation. The story of Adam and Eve richly illustrates that process. Nothing has changed since that time; everyone experiences life just like Adam and Eve. The snakes of doubt continue to slither in and out of the human mind. An individual must understand that God's rules are the only rules for life. No one has the ability to play God or make the rules. That was Adam and Eve's mistake and humanity continues to repeat the same mistake.

Participants need to understand that God's love is stronger than sin and temptation. Human beings have to learn to let God handle this intrusive power; they cannot do it alone.

Preparation

Gather newsprint, markers, masking tape, pencils, Bibles, red construction paper and scissors.

Draw a large tree on newsprint and hang it on the wall. Cut out apple shapes and write on them the scripture passages from the "Temptation Apples" worksheet. Tape the apple shapes to the tree and place a marker nearby. Place Bibles on a table near the door. Tape two sheets of newsprint to the wall. Label one "Temptations: Similarities and Differences" and leave the other blank.

Session

Opening (10 minutes)—As people arrive, assign each person one of the scripture passages from the "Temptation Apples" worksheet. Ask the participants to pick up a Bible, look up their assigned passage and write the kind of temptation the passage is talking about. Passages may describe power, lying, judging and so on. If an individual finishes early, ask him or her to look up additional passages on that page.

Ask for volunteers to share their discoveries. After each passage is discussed, hand the person a marker. Ask him or her to go to the tree and write the temptation on the corresponding apple. Ask the group, "How are the temptations described in these passages similar or different from the temptations you face today?" List responses on the newsprint labeled "Temptations: Similarities and Differences."

Ask the group members to share experiences they may have had in which temptation led to disappointment. For example, a parent may have worked overtime, neglecting family and friends, to earn a special promotion and found out he or she didn't like that new position after all.

Theme presentation (15 minutes)—Tell the group: "It's obvious from the scripture passages you've just read that temptation has been here a long time. Everyone in the history of God's people has had trouble dealing with it. The reality of temptation will always be humanity's desire to go

How It All Started

(Directed Reading)

Instructions: You have been divided into seven groups. Each group has been assigned one part. Read your part aloud with the rest of your group. Try to sound like one voice as you read together.

Narrator 1: The Lord God took the man and put him in the Garden of Eden to work it and take care of it. And the Lord God commanded the man,

God: You are free to eat from any tree in the garden; but you must not eat from the tree of the knowledge of good and evil, for when you eat of it you will surely die.

Narrator 1: The Lord God said,

God: It is not good for the man to be alone. I will make a helper suitable for him.

Narrator 2: Now the Lord God had formed out of the ground all the beasts of the field and all the birds of the air. He brought them to the man to see what he would name them; and whatever the man called each living creature, that was its name. So the man gave names to all the livestock, the birds of the air and all the beasts of the field.

Narrator 3: But for Adam no suitable helper was found. So the Lord God caused the man to fall into a deep sleep; and while he was sleeping, he took one of the man's ribs and closed up the place with flesh.

Narrator 1: Then the Lord God made a woman from the rib he had taken out of the man, and he brought her to the man. The man said,

Adam: This is now bone of my bones and flesh of my flesh; she shall be called "woman," for she was taken out of man.

Narrator 2: The man and his wife were both naked, and they felt no shame.

Narrator 3: Now the serpent was more crafty than any of the wild animals the Lord God had made. He said to the woman,

Serpent: (Sly, questioning voice) Did God really say, "You must not eat from any tree in the garden"?

Eve: (Firmly) We may eat fruit from the trees in the garden, but God did say, "You must not eat fruit from the tree that is in the middle of the garden, and you must not touch it, or you will die."

Serpent: (Emphatic statement of assurance) You will not surely die! For God knows that when you eat of it your eyes will be opened, and you will be like God, knowing good and evil.

Narrator 1: When the woman saw that the fruit of the tree was good for food and pleasing to the eye, and also desirable for gaining wisdom, she took some and ate it. She also gave some to her husband, who was with her, and he ate it.

Narrator 2: Then the eyes of both of them were opened, and they realized they were naked; so they sewed fig leaves together and made coverings for themselves.

Narrator 3: Then the man and his wife heard the sound of the Lord God as he was walking in the garden in the cool of the day, and they hid from the Lord God among the trees of the garden. But the Lord God called to the man,

God: Where are you?

Adam: (Apologetic) I heard you in the garden, and I was afraid because I was naked; so I hid.

God: Who told you that you were naked? Have you eaten from the tree that I commanded you not to eat from?

Adam: (Blaming) The woman you put here with me—she gave me some fruit from the tree, and I ate it.

God: (To Eve) What is this you have done?

Eve: (Blaming) The serpent deceived me, and I ate.

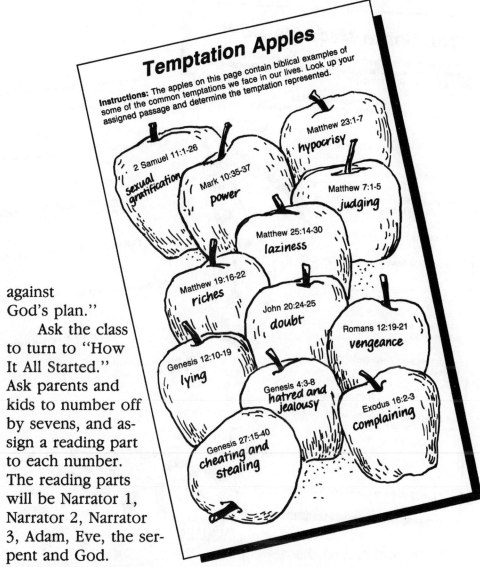

Temptation Apples

Instructions: The apples on this page contain biblical examples of some of the common temptations we face in our lives. Look up your assigned passage and determine the temptation represented.

2 Samuel 11:1-26 — *sexual gratification*

Matthew 23:1-7 — *hypocrisy*

Mark 10:35-37 — *power*

Matthew 7:1-5 — *judging*

Matthew 25:14-30 — *laziness*

Matthew 19:16-22 — *riches*

John 20:24-25 — *doubt*

Romans 12:19-21 — *vengeance*

Genesis 12:10-19 — *lying*

Genesis 4:3-8 — *hatred and jealousy*

Exodus 16:2-3 — *complaining*

Genesis 27:15-40 — *cheating and stealing*

against God's plan."

Ask the class to turn to "How It All Started." Ask parents and kids to number off by sevens, and assign a reading part to each number. The reading parts will be Narrator 1, Narrator 2, Narrator 3, Adam, Eve, the serpent and God. Each group will read its part in the script.

After the reading write the words "Serpent," "Adam" and "Eve" on the blank sheet of newsprint. Ask, "Who was responsible for the Fall of Man?" Let everyone vote and then ask, "Why did you vote the way you did?"

Exploration (15 minutes)—Ask participants to stay in their reading groups; make sure parents and kids are distributed as evenly as possible. Ask groups to turn to "The Snake Made Me Do It" worksheet. Tell them: "You are to work on the first two sections of this worksheet as a group. If your answers differ, vote on the answer your group wants

The Snake Made Me Do It

Instructions: Work as a group to complete the first two sections of this worksheet. Complete the last section on your own and discuss your answers within your small group.

Exploring the Facts

1. Does God provide Adam with everything he needs for the "good life"? Explain.

2. What is the one rule God has for Adam?

3. Does Eve understand that rule? Explain.

4. What does the serpent say to Eve to persuade her to break the rule?

5. What is Eve's reason for eating the fruit?

6. What is Adam's reason for eating it?

7. What immediately happens to Adam and Eve after they eat the fruit?

8. Who does Eve blame for falling prey to temptation?

9. Who does Adam blame for falling into temptation?

Exploring Responses

1. Why does God tell Adam and Eve they may eat everything in the garden except the fruit of the tree of knowledge?

2. What does the tree of knowledge symbolize?

3. Why do Adam and Eve become embarrassed?

4. What do Adam and Eve think they will gain by breaking God's rule?

5. Why do Adam and Eve try to find someone to blame for their actions?

Exploring the Truth About Temptation

1. Who makes you fall into temptation?

2. Why is blaming someone else an easy excuse to fall into temptation?

3. Why do you think God alone should be the author of the rules for life?

4. What are some ways you have learned to deal with temptation?

5. When you fall into temptation and go against God's plan, it means you want to make your own rules. What are some reasons for that?

6. What is wrong with the statement, "The devil made me do it"?

to use and record the decision in the blank. Complete the last section on your own."

After about 10 minutes, call the groups together. Ask if groups had trouble with any of the questions.

Response (10 minutes)—Divide the class into parents and junior highers. Ask both groups to form circles at opposite ends of the room. Have each person use the worksheet titled "I'm Only Human" to decide on the top five temptations he or she faces right now.

When participants complete their lists, ask each person

I'm Only Human

Instructions: Look over the following list of temptations junior highers and parents face daily. Pick out the five temptations that most frequently cause you problems. How do these temptations get you into trouble?

My Top Temptations	How They Get Me Into Trouble
1.	
2.	
3.	
4.	
5.	

Temptations
(If a big one in your life isn't listed, add it.)

Cheating
Breaking curfew
Yelling at people
Gossiping
Breaking the law
Using illegal drugs
Using obscene language
Being sexually immoral
Cutting people down
Lying
Being hard on brothers or sisters
Making fun of people
Being a bigot
Playing destructive pranks
Abusing others
Overeating
Not taking care of my body
Stealing
Being greedy
Being lazy
Leaving God out of my life
Hurting people physically
Dominating others
Being sarcastic
Not caring for God's creation
Wasting money
Procrastinating
Being selfish
Giving into hurtful anger
Making snap judgments

Playing unfairly
Ignoring people
Using people to get ahead
Being cruel
Being disrespectful
Complaining
Being egotistical
Not appreciating people
Not valuing what I have
Always wanting more
Grumbling
Making indignant remarks
Not willing to say "I was wrong"
Not caring about others
Being close-minded
Causing others to fall into temptation
Slandering others
Avoiding prayer
Being two-faced
Avoiding God's Word
Backstabbing
Doubting
Hating others
Being jealous
Being envious
Not sharing God's good news
Holding grudges
Being quarrelsome
Not valuing life
Wanting revenge

to share one of his or her top temptations and tell why that temptation is difficult to deal with.

Closing affirmation (5 minutes)—Ask participants to form a circle. Tell the group, "This circle signifies the group's support for each of you as you struggle with your temptations." Ask a young person to read Romans 7:18-25 and a parent to read Ephesians 6:13-18a. After these readings, tell people: "There is no magic way to keep temptation out of your life. Each of you must constantly struggle with the urge to turn away from God and create your own rules.

"Knowing that Jesus conquered temptation gives us hope that we can do the same. Paul realized we would face this dilemma when he suggested we put on God's armor. He knew God's grace is stronger than temptation. Let us all pray silently for God's grace for ourselves and for the other people in the group."

After one minute say "Amen." Remind participants to schedule their "Table Talk" time.

▀▀▀▀▀*Table Talk*▀▀▀▀▀

Instructions: "Table Talk" offers your family an opportunity to continue discussing the issue studied in class. Set aside 30 minutes for this family time.

But before you begin, remember one important thing: Practice listening as well as talking. Arguments, defensiveness, put-downs or shouting don't encourage conversation.

Now go ahead. Complete the following activity and make new discoveries about yourself and the other members of your family.

Our family "Table Talk" time this week
will be _____
TIME
DAY

Create your own Garden of Eden experience. This time you are the main character. Imagine yourself in a tempting situation such as needing the answers for a test, being too tired to go to work, knowing your parent is coming home to the messy kitchen you've just created, etc. Write a script that would take place between you and the serpent. Look back at the "How It All Started" directed reading for ideas.

My Up-to-Date Garden of Eden Experience

Narrator: (Set the scene)

Serpent: (Ask that first tempting question)

You: (Respond with what you believe is right)

Serpent: (Plant that element of doubt inside your mind)

You: (Give in to the doubt)

God: (Ask that haunting question "Did you . . . ?")

You: (Place the blame)

Explain your script to your family. Let them know the kind of support you need with the temptation you mentioned. For example, if your temptation is to talk behind a person's back, ask your family to listen to you when you are upset with a friend or another family member. Say that their tendency to give advice only deepens your anger. You *don't* need advice, you *do* need a place to vent your feelings without the message going further.

Standing firm in the face of temptation requires support from your family. Take a moment to list ways you can support each other when someone has failed to resist temptation. For example, you can reassure the person of your unconditional love. Talk about your lists.

Positive Ways to Support Each Other

1.

2.

3.

4.

5.

"Let's Talk" Questions

Instructions: Use these questions to stimulate family discussion throughout the week. An ideal time is right after dinner.

1. What is the greatest temptation a person can ever face? Why?

2. Why didn't the biblical writers try to cover up temptation?

3. What is the greatest temptation facing the world today? Explain.

4. What is the greatest temptation facing your family right now?

5. What are some ways you can help friends deal with temptation?

6. How are peer pressure and temptation related?

7. When you fall victim to temptation, why is it dangerous to say, "The devil made me do it"?

8. Do you believe there is an evil force in the world enticing people to sin? Why or why not?

9. Read 1 Corinthians 10:13: "No temptation has seized you except what is common to man. And God is faithful; he will not let you be tempted beyond what you can bear. But when you are tempted, he will also provide a way out so that you can stand up under it." *What is God's promise to you?*

What Makes Me a Winner?

"Am I okay? Do people like me? Do I have anything to offer?" These questions constantly tug at people no matter how old they are. Young people are full of these kinds of questions as they search for personal identity. Parents continue to struggle with perceived inadequacies or concerns that cripple their self-esteem.

This session looks at what it means to be a winner, both in the eyes of a secular society and within the Christian community. By using Jesus' life and words as models for success, Christians will discover that everyone can be a winner. Some just take longer to discover their winning qualities.

Objectives

During this session participants will:

● experience a simulation game that deals with winning.

● look at Jesus' life and words as the models for how to become a winner.

● affirm qualities they possess that make them winners.

Biblical Foundation

The Psalmist celebrates the value of humanity: Psalm 8

Examples of Jesus' winning qualities: Matthew 4:1-11; 5:9, 13, 16; 6:7, 19-21, 31; 7:1-5, 7-8; 8:14-17, 23-27; 9:22, 37; 11:28; 15:19-20; 16:24; 17:20; 18:4; 28:20

Background for Leader

Junior highers experience moments of extreme inadequacy. Relentless pressures from their peers batter and bruise their self-esteem. Any deviation from peers' expectations creates anxiety attacks and erodes self-esteem. Recognizing themselves as valuable is often difficult for young people. Affirming one's self-worth is critical to healthy development, both emotionally and spiritually.

Parents also live in a world of cruel expectations, except the stakes seem much higher. Loss of work and personal disappointments in the adult years can send self-esteem into a tailspin. Parents need to realize that God has equipped and empowered them to live victorious lives. Only when they recognize themselves as Christian winners can they begin to help their sons and daughters understand that affirmation.

Society constantly pressures people to be "on top." Individuals can begin to appreciate the Christian concept of self-worth only when they dismiss the secular view that a person must beat someone at something to prove his or her worth. When people use Jesus as their model for self-worth, they need no other guide to help them understand their created uniqueness.

Preparation

Gather four 3×5 cards; newsprint; two sheets of construction paper; red, blue and black markers; masking tape; pencils; Bibles and a stopwatch.

On a sheet of newsprint, copy the following "Score Sheet" and omit the extra points for the negotiation rounds. Tape the sheet to the wall.

Score Sheet

	Round	Team 1	Team 2	
	1	_____	_____	
	2	_____	_____	
Negotiate	3	_____	_____	(10 points)
	4	_____	_____	
Negotiate	5	_____	_____	(30 points)
	6	_____	_____	
Negotiate	7	_____	_____	(50 points)
	Final Totals	_____	_____	

On two of the 3×5 cards, make a large blue dot. On the other two cards, make a large red dot. Put one of each card in a set.

On two sheets of construction paper, copy the "Scoring Guidelines" for each team.

Scoring Guidelines

If both teams play a blue card: + 1 for each team
If both teams play a red card: —1 for each team
If one team plays a red card and the other team plays a blue card: + 1 for the team playing a red card
                              —1 for the team playing a blue card

Session

Opening (20 minutes)—Have all young people sit in a circle at one end of the room and all parents sit in a circle at the other end of the room. Announce to the group: "Today we will begin this session by playing the game 'Red or Blue.' Kids, you will play against your parents. The object of this game is for each team to win as many points as it can."

Hand each team a set of cards. Explain: "Each team will receive two cards, one with a blue dot and one with a red dot. Your team can win or lose points depending upon which card you choose to play in each round of the game. Select a spokesperson for your group."

After each team has selected its spokesperson, hand that individual a copy of the "Scoring Guidelines." Say: "Look at the 'Scoring Guidelines' and we'll go through them together." Read the guidelines through once.

Turn to the "Score Sheet" on the wall and explain: "This game will be played in seven rounds. During each of the seven rounds, your team will have 45 seconds to decide which card your team will play. When time is called, you will hand the card to me, I will show both cards to both teams and I will record the score. The rounds marked 'Negotiate' will offer an opportunity to gain extra points. On these rounds, send a member of your team to negotiate with a member from the other team before those extra-point rounds are played. Negotiators will leave the room to talk for 30 seconds before they report back to their own teams. Then the teams will have the normal 45 seconds to make their decisions. Remember, negotiations are not binding. If your team doesn't agree, it can alter the negotiation."

Ask the teams if they have any questions. Answer only questions about procedure. Respond to questions about the philosophy of the game by saying: "The object of this game is to win as many points as you can."

Tell the teams to prepare to play Round 1. Remind the teams they must hand in either a blue or a red card at the end of 45 seconds. Start the stopwatch. Call time after 45 seconds and collect the cards from each team. Record the scores on the "Score Sheet" and return the cards to their teams. Announce the beginning of the next round and play the same way through the game.

Prior to Rounds 3, 5 and 7, remind the teams to send their negotiators out of the room. Don't tell the teams how much these rounds are worth until after negotiations are over. Once negotiators return, announce the value of the round and allow the teams time to make their decisions. Call for the cards, show both cards to both teams and tally the scores. On the extra-point rounds, use the 10 points exactly as the one point in a normal match. For example, if both teams play a blue card, both teams earn 10 points. If both teams play a red card, both teams lose 10 points. If one plays red and one plays blue, the team playing the red card gets 10 points and the team playing the blue card loses 10 points. Total the scores as they accumulate from round to round. When the game is over, both teams may have negative numbers. Use the following questions to discuss this experience:

    1. How do you feel right now?

    2. How many points did your team win?

    3. What was the object of the game?

    4. Did anyone on your team realize that both teams had to play the blue card all the way through to win as much as possible? (Announce that if both teams had played blue all the way through, each team would have gained 95

points.)

    5. Did people on your team get frustrated? Why?

    6. What happened during the negotiations?

    7. Did your team cheat on your negotiation agreements? Why?

    8. What does this game tell us about ourselves?

    9. Why does our society demand that a winner must beat someone else at something?

    10. How does this domineering attitude affect the rest of the world?

    11. What happens to everyone's self-esteem when being a winner means beating someone at something?

    12. What does it mean to be a winner?

Theme presentation (5 minutes)—Divide the parents into four smaller groups. Do the same with the kids. Mix a group of parents and kids together to form a total of four small groups. Say: "Jesus' life presents an alternative to the kind of winning drive that society creates in us. We are going to look at his life and words as models for a winning style that has nothing to do with beating anyone at anything."

Exploration (15 minutes)—Ask participants to turn to the worksheet "Jesus, How Can I Be a Winner?" Say: "We're going to discover more about Jesus' ideas for being a winner by completing this worksheet. What does it mean to be a winner? Does being a winner mean you are the person who wins the game? Does being a winner mean you are the best student in your class? Does being a winner mean you have certain possessions? Who can answer these questions for you?

"For the Christian, being a winner means identifying with Jesus' life and ministry. This man was the greatest winner the world will ever know. Yet, what did he win? He didn't come in first in any popularity contests. He didn't win any races or competitions. In fact, many people thought Jesus was a loser, especially when he was executed as a common criminal."

Distribute Bibles. Assign a set of five questions to each small group. Give the groups five minutes to explore and find answers to their assigned questions. Ask each group to select one person to report its findings.

Jesus, How Can I Be a Winner?

Instructions: Fill in the following blanks to get a picture of what it takes to be a winner in Jesus' eyes.

1. Jesus experienced _temptation_ and knows a lot about it (Matthew 4:1-11).

2. Jesus tells us not to _babble_ when we pray (Matthew 6:7).

3. Jesus tells us to _ask_, _seek_ and _knock_ (Matthew 7:7-8).

4. Jesus says there is always a need for more _workers_ (Matthew 9:37).

5. Jesus says if we want to follow him we must be willing to _deny_ ourselves (Matthew 16:24).

6. Jesus tells us the sons of God are the _peacemakers_ (Matthew 5:9).

7. Jesus says not to lay up _treasures_ on earth (Matthew 6:19-21).

8. Jesus _heals_ others (Matthew 8:14-17).

9. Jesus says to come to him and he will give us _rest_ (Matthew 11:28).

10. Jesus tells us that we must _humble ourselves_ before we can be the greatest in the kingdom (Matthew 18:4).

11. Jesus says we are to be the _salt of the earth_ (Matthew 5:13).

12. Jesus never _judges_ others unfairly (Matthew 7:1-3).

13. Jesus has the power to _calm_ storms (Matthew 8:23-27).

14. Jesus says even if our faith is as small as a _mustard seed_ we can move mountains (Matthew 17:20).

15. Jesus tells us to _teach_ everyone to obey what he commands (Matthew 28:20).

16. Jesus tells us to let our _light shine before men_ (Matthew 5:16).

17. Jesus is someone we can never call a _hypocrite_ (Matthew 7:3-5).

18. Jesus says all we need to be made well is _faith_ (Matthew 9:22).

19. Jesus says the things that make a person unclean come from the _heart_ (Matthew 15:19-20).

20. Jesus tells us not to _worry_ (Matthew 6:31).

Bring the groups back together, and have each group report on their passages. Instruct participants to record all answers on their worksheets. After the reports, ask participants to point out Jesus' ideas of winning qualities. Remind the groups: "All these qualities are available for each one of you. Jesus said you would do even greater things than he did. You are a winner because of Christ. Follow his instruction and role modeling. Nothing else society offers comes close to the experience of living your life in him."

Response (10 minutes)—Ask participants to turn to the

"Winners Trophy" worksheet. For the next five minutes have them list five Christian qualities they possess that make them winners. People might list characteristics like kindness, compassion, honesty or sincerity.

When individuals finish, ask them to meet in family units to share the qualities they listed.

Closing affirmation (5 minutes)—Have families read Psalm 8 together. Tell the group: "God created each of you with unique and wonderful gifts and talents. When you try to base your self-worth on being a winner in society's eyes, you are bound to come up short. Only Jesus can provide the model for a winning life."

Ask individuals to close this session by affirming each family member for ways he or she is a winner. Remind families to schedule their "Table Talk" time and pray for each other as they seek to affirm their self-worth.

Winners Trophy

Instructions: You are a winner and this trophy is for you. Write your name in the space provided. In the numbered spaces, list five Christian qualities you possess. Celebrate these with your family.

Winners Trophy
Given to:
_____
for sharing the qualities of . . .

1.
2.
3.
4.
5.

WINNERS TROPHY

Table Talk

Instructions: "Table Talk" offers your family an opportunity to continue discussing the issue studied in class. Set aside 30 minutes for this family time.

But before you begin, remember one important thing: Practice listening as well as talking. Arguments, defensiveness, put-downs or shouting don't encourage conversation.

Now go ahead. Complete the following activity and make new discoveries about yourself and the other members of your family.

Our family "Table Talk" time this week will be _____
_____
TIME
DAY

Gather one sheet of paper for each family member. Write an appreciation letter to each person by following this outline:

Dear _____:
The three things I appreciate about you most are:

1.

2.

3.

You are a winner to me because _____
_____

Signed: _____

After family members have completed their letters, share your responses with one another. Put one family member in the center of the room and have the others read their letters to that person. Do this with each person.

After everyone has listened to his or her letters, talk about why it's difficult to affirm one another. List some positive steps you can take to help build each family member's self-esteem. Share your ideas with the rest of your family.

Positive Steps to Build Self-Esteem

5.

Write your name on a small piece of paper and put it in the center of the table. Have each family member draw a name, but keep it secret from the others. During this week you will be responsible for helping the person whose name you drew build his or her self-esteem. Create pleasant surprises that help to make that person feel good. Place a cookie and a glass of milk on his or her desk after school. Write him or her a note of appreciation and tape it to the mirror. Identify yourself as that person's esteem-builder at the end of the week.

"Let's Talk" Questions

Instructions: Use these questions to stimulate family discussion throughout the week. An ideal time is right after dinner.

1. Why do people sometimes feel they have no talents?

2. When you feel worthless, what are you saying to God?

3. Name some people you know who have poor self-esteem. How could you help them right now?

4. Who do you think are some winners in God's eyes?

Forgiveness Is So Hard

*F*orgiveness is hard to give and receive. When wronged, junior highers may hold vicious grudges that block forgiveness. When they disobey their parents or wrong others, junior highers may not understand how to ask for and receive forgiveness. Parents experience similar situations. They may hold grudges or verbalize their hurt through angry words. Some parents find it especially difficult to ask their children, "Will you forgive me?"

This session explores the concept of forgiveness. Through Christ we have been forgiven. This frees us to give and receive forgiveness and to forgive ourselves. Families grow closer as they learn the process of loving each other unconditionally.

Objectives

During this session participants will:
- examine the current state of forgiveness in their lives.
- reflect on their views of forgiveness.
- explore a biblical model of forgiveness.
- make decisions on initiating and receiving forgiveness.

Biblical Foundation

A forgiven servant refuses to grant forgiveness: Matthew 18:21-35

Jesus talks about forgiveness: Luke 6:37-38

A father forgives his son: Luke 15:11-32

Jesus forgives his crucifiers: Luke 23:34
Forgiving as Christ has forgiven: Ephesians 4:31-32
Forgiving as God forgives: Colossians 3:12-13

Background for Leader

The Bible depicts heroes of faith who stumbled through life and at times fell flat on their faces. God's mercy and forgiveness seem almost incomprehensible to us in light of their foolish acts. Thankfully, God's vision for forgiveness doesn't depend on our opinions and actions.

Parents and junior highers struggle with forgiveness. They ache inside when others don't forgive them. Guilt encompasses them when they hurt other family members and can't forgive themselves. Grudges may clash and grow into obsessive anger and revenge. From any angle forgiveness is difficult.

God's model of forgiveness is our blueprint of hope. We can avoid the horrible pits of guilt and revenge by following Christ's example and learning that forgiveness takes time.

In *Putting Forgiveness Into Practice*, Doris Donnelly presents five points about God's forgiveness:

1. God's forgiveness is a gift.
2. God's forgiveness involves repentance.
3. God's forgiveness involves confession.
4. God's forgiveness is powerful.
5. God's forgiveness is ours to share.

Think about these aspects before you begin this session. Remember that God forgives swiftly and completely, but forgiveness between people is a process. Donnelly expresses this process through the following steps:

1. Acknowledge your hurt; affirm the pain you feel.
2. Decide you want to forgive; decide to carry through the act of forgiveness.
3. Remember that forgiveness is a journey which takes time.
4. Remember that forgiveness isn't easy.
5. Listen to what others say about forgiveness.
6. Forgive yourself.
7. Look at the person who hurt you in a new light.

Preparation

Gather pencils, markers, Bibles, newsprint, two balls of
yarn, tape and two tables. Assign a parent to facilitate discussion for the "My View of Forgiveness" questions.

Tape a blank sheet of newsprint to the wall in front of
the room. Lay one long sheet of newsprint labeled "Steps a
Christian Should Take to Share Forgiveness" on one table,
and on the other table lay a long sheet of newsprint labeled
"Steps a Christian Should Take to Receive Forgiveness."
Place markers on the tables. Arrange chairs in two separate
circles.

Session

Opening (10 minutes)—As each person arrives, ask him
or her to sit in one or the other circle of chairs. After everyone arrives, each circle should have the same number of
people. (Form one circle if your group is smaller than 10.)
Give each circle a ball of yarn. Say: "Forgiveness is God's
free gift to you. Sometimes, however, forgiving others may
make you squirm because it doesn't always come naturally.

"Let the person who holds the ball of yarn complete
the sentence 'It's hard to forgive when . . .' For example,
you could say, 'It's hard to forgive when a person talks
about me behind my back.'

"Then hold the end of the yarn and toss the ball to
another person. He or she should complete the sentence,
hold on to the yarn and toss the ball to someone else. After
everyone completes the sentence, you'll see a tangled web
of yarn within the circle."

After participants finish making the web, say: "When
you're wronged by someone and feel hurt, it's easy to hold
a grudge. Lack of forgiveness feels like a tangled web of
knotted emotions. Think about this feeling. Then one at a
time complete the sentence 'Forgiveness is . . .' For example,
you could say, 'Forgiveness is letting go of bitter feelings.'
As you complete the sentence, drop your yarn."

After participants do this, say: "When you forgive
someone, you let go of grudges and bitterness. You say 'It's
okay' and really mean it."

Have the members move their chairs into one circle and discuss these questions:

1. Is it difficult to forgive others? Why or why not?
2. Is it difficult to forgive yourself? Why or why not?
3. Have you ever experienced a lack of forgiveness from someone else? If so, how did it feel?

Theme presentation (15 minutes)—Explain: "Struggles with forgiveness can result from confusion about how to react in certain situations. Knowing what you think about forgiveness and discussing your opinions will help you learn why it's difficult to forgive."

Distribute pencils, then ask the group to turn to "My View of Forgiveness." Ask participants to separate into young people and parents and each complete the poll. Have the assigned parent direct the questions at the end of the worksheet in the parents' group. You will help the junior highers.

After 10 minutes bring the groups back together. Ask, "What did you discover about your opinions on forgiveness?" List some of their responses on newsprint. Highlight the similarities and differences of opinion between parents and junior highers.

Exploration (15 minutes)—Divide the class into mixed groups of young people and parents by first asking the junior highers to say "prodigal, son, prodigal, son" and so on. Have the parents do the same. Then ask all "prodigals" to form one group and all "sons" to form another.

Distribute Bibles, then ask individuals to turn to "Exploring the Prodigal Son Story." Tell them to read the story in their Bibles and then discuss the questions in their small groups.

After 10 minutes gather the groups and share their discoveries.

Response (10 minutes)—Read the two statements on the long sheets of newsprint placed on the two tables: "Steps a Christian Should Take to Share Forgiveness" and "Steps a Christian Should Take to Receive Forgiveness."

Ask the group members to think of ways to answer the statements. As they generate ideas, have them draw footprints on the newsprint. Ask them to write the "steps" to sharing or receiving forgiveness inside the footprints. Use

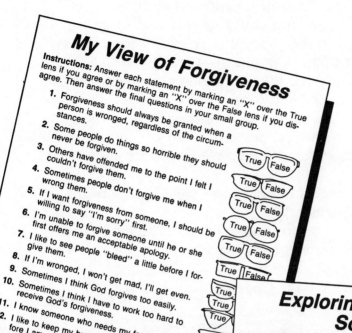

My View of Forgiveness

Instructions: Answer each statement by marking an "X" over the True lens if you agree or by marking an "X" over the False lens if you disagree. Then answer the final questions in your small group.

1. Forgiveness should always be granted when a person is wronged, regardless of the circumstances.
2. Some people do things so horrible they should never be forgiven.
3. Others have offended me to the point I felt I couldn't forgive them.
4. Sometimes people don't forgive me when I wrong them.
5. If I want forgiveness from someone, I should be willing to say "I'm sorry" first.
6. I'm unable to forgive someone until he or she first offers me an acceptable apology.
7. I like to see people "bleed" a little before I forgive them.
8. If I'm wronged, I won't get mad, I'll get even.
9. Sometimes I think God forgives too easily.
10. Sometimes I think I have to work too hard to receive God's forgiveness.
11. I know someone who needs my forgiveness.
12. I like to keep my hurt and anger for a while before I am ready to forgive.
13. There are some things I could do that God wouldn't forgive me for.
14. I know someone I need forgiveness from.
15. I have trouble forgiving myself when I hurt someone on purpose.
16. My family needs to talk about forgiveness in certain areas.
17. A Christian must always be willing to give and receive forgiveness.

Discussion Questions
1. What statements in the poll did you agree with? disagree with? Explain.
2. What did you discover about your opinions on forgiveness?
3. Which do you have more trouble with: giving forgiveness or accepting forgiveness? Explain.

Exploring the Prodigal Son Story

Instructions: Read Luke 15:11-24, then discuss the questions in your small group.

The Basics
1. What does the son demand from his father? What does the father do?
2. Where does the son go? What happens there?
3. Why does the son change his mind? What does the father do when the son comes home?

Opinions
1. Why does the son want to leave home?
2. If you were the father, how would you feel if your son demanded his inheritance and left home?
3. What does the son discover about life while living in the distant country?
4. If you were the father, how would you react if your son came back home?

More Opinions
1. Why do you think Jesus told this parable?
2. When have you acted like the prodigal son? the forgiving father?
3. Who does the father represent? the son? Explain.
4. When was the last time you received forgiveness from someone?

the Background for Leader information to facilitate responses. For example, you could suggest that forgiving yourself is one step in the process of receiving forgiveness.

Closing affirmation (5 minutes)—Close by saying: "Jesus is our model of the ideal forgiving person. He was always sincere; he never faked forgiveness. Jesus accepted all people for who they were. He always tried to love them into a relationship with God. Jesus reached out in forgiveness even when he suffered the cruelest injustice of all—the cross."

Ask three volunteers to read Luke 6:37-38; Ephesians 4:31-32; and Colossians 3:12-13

Say: "God calls you to forgive others. The family is a crucial area for forgiveness to take place. Many times learning how to forgive begins at home. Turn to the 'Certificates of Forgiveness.' Fill in the name of one person you need to forgive and one person you need forgiveness from. If needed, put family names first. Show each certificate to the person named sometime this week."

Ask each family to join hands and take turns declaring their appreciation to God for each member. Remind families to schedule this week's "Table Talk" time.

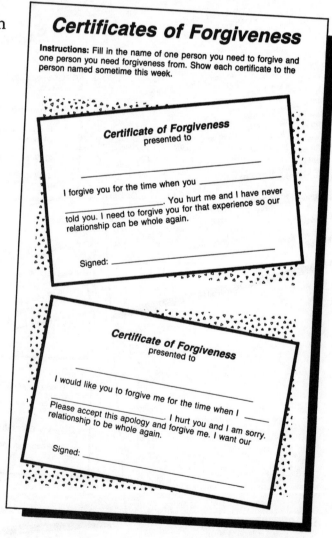

Certificates of Forgiveness

Instructions: Fill in the name of one person you need to forgive and one person you need forgiveness from. Show each certificate to the person named sometime this week.

Certificate of Forgiveness
presented to

_____

I forgive you for the time when you _____
_____. You hurt me and I have never told you. I need to forgive you for that experience so our relationship can be whole again.

Signed: _____

Certificate of Forgiveness
presented to

I would like you to forgive me for the time when I ____
_____. I hurt you and I am sorry. Please accept this apology and forgive me. I want our relationship to be whole again.

Signed: _____

▰▰▰▰*Table Talk*▰▰▰▰

Instructions: "Table Talk" offers your family an opportunity to continue discussing the issue studied in class. Set aside 30 minutes for this family time.

But before you begin, remember one important thing: Practice listening as well as talking. Arguments, defensiveness, put-downs or shouting don't encourage conversation.

Now go ahead. Complete the following activity and make new discoveries about yourself and the other members of your family.

Our family "Table Talk" time this week will be _____
TIME
DAY

Think about the last time a family member forgave you and the last time you forgave a family member. Describe both instances in the space provided.

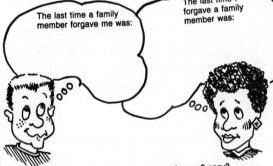

The last time a family member forgave me was:

The last time I forgave a family member was:

1. In what ways is forgiveness difficult for you? easy?

2. Is there someone in the family you need to forgive right now? Explain.

3. Is there someone in the family you need forgiveness from? Explain.

...ttled needs for forgiveness. If so, list your ...x.

My Needs for Forgiveness

Deal with those needs right now. Discuss all the issues with your family. Decide how to begin to heal the hurt and pain.

"Let's Talk" Questions

Instructions: Use these questions to stimulate family discussion throughout the week. An ideal time is right after dinner.

1. Why is it so difficult to forgive those who wrong us?

2. What do you think Jesus felt about forgiveness?

3. What does our world need to learn about forgiveness? (Read Luke 6:37-38.)

4. What is one attitude about forgiveness you need to change?

5. What are the benefits to you for forgiving someone?

Bridges to Trust

"**Y**ou don't trust me!" echoes at one time or another through the homes of parents and adolescents. Trust is one of the piercing points of contention between parents and their young people. Only time builds trust, yet it is nurtured by openness and mutual respect.

Why is trust important anyway? What does biblical history teach about trust? How can families create a climate where trust will bloom? How can a relationship with Christ help individuals develop trust in one another? This session explores numerous questions about trust.

Objectives

During this session participants will:
- experience what it means to be a part of a trustful relationship.
- evaluate how trusting they are.
- look at biblical models of trust.
- discuss what builds up or tears down trust within relationships.

Biblical Foundation

God calls Abram to move: Genesis 12:1-4

God calls Moses to rescue his people from Egypt: Exodus 3:7-12; 4:18-20; 5:1

David recognizes God's presence when he stands up to the Philistine: 1 Samuel 17:41-50

Elijah challenges the prophets of Baal: 1 Kings 18:20-40

The centurion trusts Jesus' words alone: Matthew 8:5-10

The disciples follow Jesus: Mark 1:16-20

Friends of the paralytic lower him through the roof to Jesus: Mark 2:1-5

The woman is healed as she touches Jesus' cloak: Mark 5:25-34

Background for Leader

Trust may be faith's ultimate test. To put oneself in Jesus' hands with the confidence that he will provide guidance seems risky at first. It's much like having someone put their confidence in you for the first time and telling you, "I know you won't let me down." When you put your confidence in someone, you believe that he or she will come through.

When lack of trust erodes family relationships, parents and adolescents wrestle in turmoil and conflict. They fling accusations, hoping to inflict pain on those who have disappointed them. Families can have fierce battles when egos clash over who's responsible for the latest breakdown of trust.

Without trust, a family cannot support each other in a climate of love and nurture. Suspicion creeps in like a fog to distort each person's view. Family members need to do everything they can to battle the fog and restore trust with each other.

Encourage participants to be honest with themselves. Ask them to think seriously about what they do to foster or destroy trust in their families and other relationships. Jesus exemplifies the lifestyle of a trust builder, not a trust breaker. Through him, everyone can experience God's unconditional trust and love. Trusting others and being trustworthy are two complementary positions on which to build good family relationships.

Preparation

Gather newsprint, markers, pencils, masking tape, 3×5 cards, Bibles, a whistle and blindfolds for half the group.

Copy this scoring diagram on newsprint, tape it to the wall and cover it with another sheet of newsprint.

How Trusting or Trustworthy Am I?

12-15 = I am exceptionally trustworthy and trusting with others.

8-11 = Normally I am trustworthy and have little trouble

trusting others.

4-7 = I have trouble with some areas of trust.

0-3 = Hey, trust just "isn't my thing."

Set up an obstacle course in another room. Scatter two or three chairs throughout the room. Put a table at one end of the room for people to walk around. Tape a blanket or sheet to the floor for people to walk on. Hang strings from the ceiling for people to walk through. Make the course easy and safe. If you have no room for this activity inside, go outside.

On long sheets of newsprint, prepare two copies of the following diagram and tape them at opposite ends of the meeting room. Place a marker near each diagram.

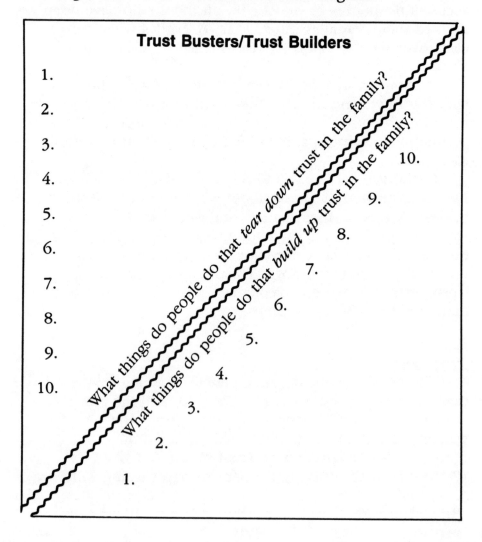

Session

Opening (10 minutes)—As people arrive, have them turn to the "How Trusting or Trustworthy Am I?" worksheet. Ask them to read the questionnaire, circle their responses and figure their totals at the bottom of the page.

Uncover the scoring diagram for the questionnaire and have group members compare only the total of their Yes responses with the scoring diagram. Discuss the following questions:

1. Why did you respond to the questions the way you did?

2. If you have a high score, why do you think you are so trusting or trustworthy?

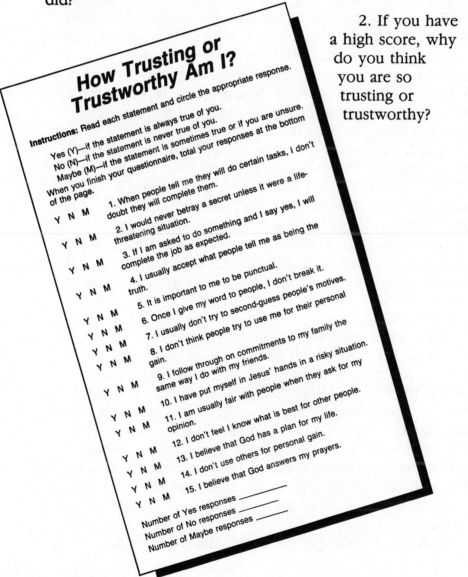

How Trusting or Trustworthy Am I?

Instructions: Read each statement and circle the appropriate response.

Yes (Y)—if the statement is always true of you.
No (N)—if the statement is never true of you.
Maybe (M)—if the statement is sometimes true or if you are unsure.
When you finish your questionnaire, total your responses at the bottom of the page.

Y N M   1. When people tell me they will do certain tasks, I don't doubt they will complete them.

Y N M   2. I would never betray a secret unless it were a life-threatening situation.

Y N M   3. If I am asked to do something and I say yes, I will complete the job as expected.

Y N M   4. I usually accept what people tell me as being the truth.

Y N M   5. It is important to me to be punctual.

Y N M   6. Once I give my word to people, I don't break it.

Y N M   7. I usually don't try to second-guess people's motives.

Y N M   8. I don't think people try to use me for their personal gain.

Y N M   9. I follow through on commitments to my family the same way I do with my friends.

Y N M   10. I have put myself in Jesus' hands in a risky situation.

Y N M   11. I am usually fair with people when they ask for my opinion.

Y N M   12. I don't feel I know what is best for other people.

Y N M   13. I believe that God has a plan for my life.

Y N M   14. I don't use others for personal gain.

Y N M   15. I believe that God answers my prayers.

Number of Yes responses _____
Number of No responses _____
Number of Maybe responses _____

3. If you have a low score, why do you think you have a low trust level right now?

4. Were you surprised by what you learned about your trust level? Why or why not?

Theme presentation (15 minutes)—Divide the group into pairs. Try to match a junior higher with a parent as much as possible. Give each pair a blindfold and explain: "All of you will participate in a three-stage trust walk. One person in each pair will be blindfolded. The blindfolded people will rely solely on their sighted partners to guide them so they won't run into something along the way.

"This three-minute trust walk will have three stages. During the first minute, sighted people may speak to and touch their blindfolded partners. When the whistle blows to start the second minute, sighted people may no longer speak, but will continue to guide their partners by touch. When the whistle blows for the third minute, sighted people can no longer touch their blindfolded partners. They must talk them through the rest of the walk."

Ask if there are any questions. Tell participants you will remind them of the requirements each time you blow the whistle. Have the group follow you to the room with the obstacle course. Have the person holding the blindfold help his or her partner put on the blindfold. Once every pair is ready, tell the group: "Turn your blindfolded partners around several times and distribute yourselves throughout the room. When I blow the whistle, begin." Each time you blow the whistle, remind the group members of what they should be doing.

After three minutes have participants remove their blindfolds. Say: "Now you get to reverse your position; those of you who were blindfolded get to become the leaders. Help your partners put on the blindfolds while I rearrange the obstacle course." Make noises as if you were creating large changes, but keep basically the same course. Tell the group, "Turn your blindfolded partners around several times and lead them to a new position in the room." Blow your whistle to begin; each time you blow the whistle, give a brief reminder about what people should be doing.

Talk about the experience with these questions:

1. How did it feel to *not* be in control of what was happening to you?

2. What do you remember about the walk when you were blindfolded?

3. What do you remember about the walk when you were the leader?

4. Which of the three parts of the trust walk was most difficult for you? Why?

5. What was the level of trust between you and your partner? Why?

6. Did you find the age difference affecting your trust level? Why or why not?

Exploration (15 minutes)—Go back to the regular meeting room. Ask each pair to find another pair to work with. Ask the small groups to turn to the "Truths for Trusting" worksheet. Pass out Bibles. Assign each group one of the

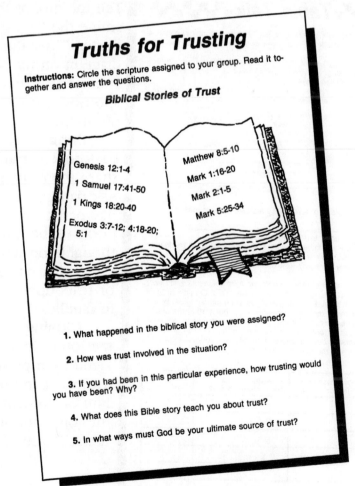

Truths for Trusting

Instructions: Circle the scripture assigned to your group. Read it together and answer the questions.

Biblical Stories of Trust

Genesis 12:1-4

1 Samuel 17:41-50

1 Kings 18:20-40

Exodus 3:7-12; 4:18-20; 5:1

Matthew 8:5-10

Mark 1:16-20

Mark 2:1-5

Mark 5:25-34

1. What happened in the biblical story you were assigned?

2. How was trust involved in the situation?

3. If you had been in this particular experience, how trusting would you have been? Why?

4. What does this Bible story teach you about trust?

5. In what ways must God be your ultimate source of trust?

biblical stories at the top of the page. Have them circle their assignments and answer the questions in relation to their assigned stories.

After everyone has finished, ask the small groups to gather and discuss the following questions:

1. What was your story about?

2. What were some of the trusting qualities of the biblical characters you read about?

3. How much do you think these biblical characters' faith had to do with their trust levels?

4. How can these reflections on biblical characters help you establish and nurture trustworthy relationships in your home?

Response (10 minutes)—Ask parents to meet at one end of the room and kids to meet at the other. Appoint a recorder in each group. Tell the groups to examine the "Trust Busters/Trust Builders" diagram on the wall and list at least 10 responses to each question.

Bring the groups back together and share the responses. Ask participants to pay particular attention to other groups' thoughts on what they think builds up or tears down trust in families.

Closing affirmation (5 minutes)—Hand each person a 3×5 card and have him or her complete the following statement: "One

Table Talk

Instructions: "Table Talk" offers your family an opportunity to continue discussing the issue studied in class. Set aside 30 minutes for this family time.

But before you begin, remember one important thing: Practice listening as well as talking. Arguments, defensiveness, put-downs or shouting don't encourage conversation.

Now go ahead. Complete the following activity and make new discoveries about yourself and the other members of your family.

Our family "Table Talk" time this week will be _____ TIME _____ DAY

Complete the following open-ended statement: Trust means _____.

Discuss your definition of trust with the rest of the family.

Write each family member's name in the first column of the following form. Think about how you relate to each person. How much do you trust each family member? How much do family members trust you?

Answer the questions in the second and third columns beside each person's name by choosing a number from the "Trust Continuum" that indicates your trust level. For example if you are a junior higher, you may feel you trust your mother completely. If so, put a 10 in the blank under the second column. If she seems to question you about some of your friends, you might put a 5 or a 6 under the third column. If you want to explain one or both of your responses, write your reasons in the last column under the question "Why?"

Family members	How much do I trust him or her?	How much does he or she trust me?	Why?

commitment I will make to help build trust in my family will be to . . ." Ask each person to meet with his or her family members to share responses on the cards. After everyone has shared, close this time with each person praying silently for the strength to fulfill his or her commitment to the rest of the family.

Challenge participants to model Christian attitudes that allow people to trust them and for them to trust others. Tell the group: "Trust is proportional; when one receives trust from others, it is much easier to offer trust in return."

Remind families to schedule their "Table Talk" time. Dismiss the group by reading the following scripture passage: "Trust in the Lord and do good; dwell in the land and enjoy safe pasture. Delight yourself in the Lord and he will give you the desires of your heart" (Psalm 37:3-4).

Trust Continuum

No			Sometimes							Total
0	1	2	3	4	5	6	7	8	9	10
trust				I can trust						trust

Share your responses with the rest of the family. Be open and honest with one another. Talk about why trust levels might vary between family members.

After your discussion, complete the following statement: If I could choose only one thing to happen in our family so we could build more trust among us, I would like _____

_____.

Share your idea with the rest of the family. Work together to list five things your family can do to build more trust.

1.

2.

3.

4.

5.

Think about what you can do when trust levels start to erode. Set up a family plan for dealing with trust issues when they arise. Complete the following statement: When trust levels in my family begin to deteriorate, I will _____

_____.

"Let's Talk" Questions

Instructions: Use these questions to stimulate family discussion throughout the week. An ideal time is right after dinner.

1. Why do people from different cultures seem to have difficulty trusting each other?

2. Why is it hard to start trusting someone again once he or she has betrayed you?

3. What would you want a person to do if you had betrayed his or her trust?

4. What biblical personalities do you think were most trusting? Why?

5. What one thing tears down trust the most? Explain.

6. What one thing builds up trust the most? Explain.

Putting Compassion to Work

Everyone needs compassion. Individuals cannot live without this kind of nourishment, no matter how old they are.

Jesus was a powerful model of compassion. Using his life as a guide, this session helps parents and junior highers accept and be more compassionate with one another.

Objectives

During this session participants will:
- look at ways Jesus showed compassion for people.
- evaluate personal levels of compassion.
- decide which characteristics of love they share with their families.
- list ways they can show compassion to others.

Biblical Foundation

Jesus and Paul explain how to live compassionately:

Luke 10:30-35
Romans 12:3, 9-10, 16-18
Galatians 5:22-23, 25-26; 6:2, 7-9
Ephesians 4:1-3, 29, 31-32
Philippians 2:3-4
Colossians 3:12-15

Background for Leader

Society seems to be rationing its supply of compassion these days. The old standard of seven hugs a day has eroded into seven hugs a week for the lucky ones. Individuals find it more and more difficult to demonstrate compassion to others when they are in desperate need themselves. Billboards and advertisements push people to live life to the fullest. So while society keeps individuals "doing their own thing," they lose track of opportunities for expressing their warmth, care and kindness to others.

Compassion was another of Jesus' gifts. Everywhere he went he touched people with his love. Healing, listening, accepting and responding were all part of Jesus' ministry.

Parents and young people can use Jesus' model of love as the foundation for compassion within their homes. When they see how Jesus demonstrated his care and concern, families will begin to understand how expressing or withholding compassion can affect their lives. They will feel challenged to flavor their relationships with compassion so acceptance and appreciation will prevail.

Preparation

Gather newsprint, masking tape, pencils and markers.

Write this statement on newsprint and tape it to the wall: "People Show They Care About Me When They . . ." During the opening brainstorming session, play music that addresses ways people indicate they care about others. For example, Stevie Wonder's "I Just Called to Say I Love You" reflects this care.

On a separate sheet of newsprint, copy the following scoring outline for the survey titled "Your Emotional Thermometer."

Emotional Temperature
64-80 = Extreme compassion.
48-63 = Very caring.
32-47 = Some things move me, some things don't.
16-31 = May need an emotional transfusion.

Cover the outline with a blank piece of newsprint until you are ready to use it in the Response section.

Session

Opening (10 minutes)—As people arrive, divide them into small groups of four or five people. Give each group a sheet of newsprint and a marker. Tell participants to brainstorm a list of at least 20 things people do to show they love or care about someone.

Bring the groups together. Tape each group's newsprint on the wall and ask one person from each group to share its list. Place a star next to ideas that are on more than one list. After every group has shared ask, "With all these good ideas, why is it so hard for people to be compassionate and caring in our world today?"

Theme presentation (10 minutes)—Tell group members to turn to "A Look at the Good Samaritan." Say: "We are going to look at a biblical model of compassion. Break into small groups with three or four people seated near you and

A Look at the Good Samaritan

Instructions: Read the following scripture passage and discuss the questions.

In reply Jesus said: "A man was going down from Jerusalem to Jericho, when he fell into the hands of robbers. They stripped him of his clothes, beat him and went away, leaving him half dead. A priest happened to be going down the same road, and when he saw the man, he passed by on the other side. So too, a Levite, when he came to the place and saw him, passed by on the other side. But a Samaritan, as he traveled, came where the man was; and when he saw him, he took pity on him. He went to him and bandaged his wounds, pouring on oil and wine. Then he put the man on his own donkey, took him to an inn and took care of him. The next day he took out two silver coins and gave them to the innkeeper. 'Look after him,' he said, 'and when I return, I will reimburse you for any extra expense you may have'" (Luke 10:30-35).

Discussion Questions

1. What did each of the characters in the parable do?

2. What are some reasons the priest and Levite might not have wanted to help?

3. How much help did the Samaritan give?

4. If you had been the Samaritan, how much help would you have offered?

5. Why do you think Jesus told this parable?

6. When have you extended an act of compassion to someone recently?

7. When has someone extended an act of compassion to you recently?

8. When have you acted as the "good Samaritan" in your family?

Family Love Review

Instructions: Read the following scripture passage. Then read each of the "Love Reviews." Rate yourself, from 1 to 10 on how much you share that quality of love with your family (1 = never; 10 = always).

> Love is patient, love is kind. It does not envy, it does not boast, it is not proud. It is not rude, it is not self-seeking, it is not easily angered, it keeps no record of wrongs. Love does not delight in evil but rejoices with the truth. It always protects, always trusts, always hopes, always perseveres (1 Corinthians 13:4-7).

Love Reviews

Love is patient.
I am patient with family members. I try to see their side of issues and seek to understand their motives for doing or saying something. I am slow to get angry and I never yell at family members.
Never   1   2   3   4   5   6   7   8   9   10   Always

Love is kind.
I am thoughtful and caring toward family members. I offer encouragement and try to build family members up. I appreciate what they do for me and I let them know that.
Never   1   2   3   4   5   6   7   8   9   10   Always

Love does not envy.
I don't get upset when someone else in the family receives something I don't. I don't get angry when another family member succeeds and I don't. I don't keep a running score on who gets what and demand my equal share.
Never   1   2   3   4   5   6   7   8   9   10   Always

Love does not boast.
I don't try to be the most important person in my family. I don't want excess attention nor do I expect to be showered by special treatment because I feel I'm the most important person in the family. I work to help all of my family feel important.
Never   1   2   3   4   5   6   7   8   9   10   Always

Love is not proud.
I try to understand my limitations. I don't let my ego determine how I act or react to family members. I don't put down other family members when they don't measure up to my expectations.
Never   1   2   3   4   5 ...

Love is not rude.
I don't use sarcasm and biting comments in the family. I don't deliberately hurt family members with my language or actions. I try to support family members in all I do.
Never   1   2   3   4   5   6   7   8   9   10   Always

Love is not self-seeking.
I don't try to make the family conform to my ways of doing things. I don't make demands on other family members just to ease my lifestyle.
Never   1   2   3   4   5   6   7   8   9   10   Always

Love is not easily angered.
I don't have a supersensitive attitude that makes the rest of my family walk on eggshells when they are around me. I don't intentionally irritate other family members. I try to be easygoing with my family.
Never   1   2   3   4   5   6   7   8   9   10   Always

Love doesn't remember wrongs.
I have learned how important forgiveness is in my family, and I forgive freely. I don't hold grudges, and I don't belittle other family members' mistakes.
Never   1   2   3   4   5   6   7   8   9   10   Always

Love rejoices in truth, not evil.
I don't delight in another family member's failure, even when it makes me look good. When facing tough family times, I try to be a source of emotional encouragement.
Never   1   2   3   4   5   6   7   8   9   10   Always

Love always perseveres.
When I become angry with a family member, I never give up on our relationship. I know we can work out our difficulties. I keep talking and letting that person know I care, regardless of how that family member treats me.
Never   1   2   3   4   5   6   7   8   9   10   Always

Your Emotional Thermometer

Instructions: Look over the following situations. Rate yourself from 1 to 5 based on how much emotion you feel that situation would generate in you (1 = no emotion; 5 = extreme emotion).

1. Seeing a blind person struggling to get across a busy street.
1 — 2 — 3 — 4 — 5

2. Watching a TV documentary of children starving to death in Africa.
1 — 2 — 3 — 4 — 5

3. Going to see a heartbreaking movie.
1 — 2 — 3 — 4 — 5

4. Sitting with a close friend whose loved one has just died.
1 — 2 — 3 — 4 — 5

5. Finding your pet run over in the street.
1 — 2 — 3 — 4 — 5

6. Seeing a friend work hard for something and then not get it.
1 — 2 — 3 — 4 — 5

7. Talking with a family member who is experiencing some hard struggles.
1 — 2 — 3 — 4 — 5

8. Having a beggar come to your door to ask for food and help with finding a place to stay.
1 — 2 — 3 — 4 — 5

9. Talking with a close friend who has just experienced an end to an important relationship.
1 — 2 — 3 — 4 — 5

10. Witnessing a situation where a person is being ridiculed.
1 — 2 — 3 — 4 — 5

11. Leaving a situation where you have just hurt someone's feelings.
1 — 2 — 3 — 4 — 5

12. Hearing an announcement that a horrible disaster has just occurred.
1 — 2 — 3 — 4 — 5

13. Reading an emotion-packed book.
1 — 2 — 3 — 4 — 5

14. Watching a TV interview of a victim of a terrible crime.
1 — 2 — 3 — 4 — 5

15. Being told a close family member has just died.
1 — 2 — 3 — 4 — 5

16. Finding out a close friend has been injured in a traffic accident.
1 — 2 — 3 — 4 — 5

Add all the numbers you circled. My emotional temperature is: _____.

read the scripture passage at the top of your worksheet. Then answer the questions."

After about five minutes, gather the groups and discuss the following questions:

1. When was a time this week when you were offered an act of compassion?

2. When was a time this week you offered an act of compassion?

3. Is it easier to be compassionate with members of your family or with people outside your family? Why?

Exploration (15 minutes)—Ask participants to turn to the "Family Love Review" worksheet. Say: "Paul shared some important qualities about love in 1 Corinthians 13:4-7. They provide a foundation for compassionate responses to people. Look at the list of qualities on this worksheet and rate yourself on how much you share that quality within your family."

After individuals have completed their surveys, tell them to meet with their families to talk about their responses. Tell them you will hold up your hand when it is time to proceed to the next activity.

Response (15 minutes)—Hold up your hand and make sure you have each family's attention. Say: "Each person needs to examine and recognize the level of compassion you have within. You have just examined some feelings about expressing love within your family. Now you are going to evaluate your level of emotional response to other life experiences. Turn to the worksheet titled 'Your Emotional Thermometer.' Let's read through the directions together."

Make sure there are no questions, then tell the participants: "Turn your chair to face away from your family and complete the worksheet on your own. Be sure to total your score at the bottom of the page."

After everyone has finished, uncover the scoring outline for the worksheet. Ask participants to total their points and discover their emotional temperature. Ask two or three family units to meet together to discuss the following questions:

1. What causes some people to be more compassionate than others?

2. Why do some people think of compassion as a sign of weakness?

3. What suggestions do you have for developing a more compassionate attitude toward others?

Closing affirmation (5 minutes)—Ask everyone to gather in a circle, with family members sitting next to each other. Tell participants to turn to "Paul's Building Blocks of Compassion."

Tell the group: "These building blocks were Paul's affirmations to the early church. He worked continuously to help Christ's followers learn how to care for one another. As families we need to work together to increase our capacities for compassion. To symbolize a willingness to work together, each family will read a scripture passage aloud to the rest of the group. Go around the room until all families have had a chance to read together. If there are more families than verses, your family may read one that's especially meaningful to you."

After each family has had a chance to participate, ask: "What would happen if you were to take seriously Jesus'

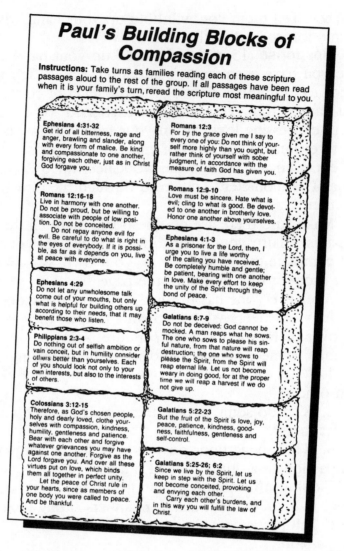

Paul's Building Blocks of Compassion

Instructions: Take turns as families reading each of these scripture passages aloud to the rest of the group. If all passages have been read when it is your family's turn, reread the scripture most meaningful to you.

Ephesians 4:31-32
Get rid of all bitterness, rage and anger, brawling and slander, along with every form of malice. Be kind and compassionate to one another, forgiving each other, just as in Christ God forgave you.

Romans 12:3
For by the grace given me I say to every one of you: Do not think of yourself more highly than you ought, but rather think of yourself with sober judgment, in accordance with the measure of faith God has given you.

Romans 12:16-18
Live in harmony with one another. Do not be proud, but be willing to associate with people of low position. Do not be conceited.
Do not repay anyone evil for evil. Be careful to do what is right in the eyes of everybody. If it is possible, as far as it depends on you, live at peace with everyone.

Romans 12:9-10
Love must be sincere. Hate what is evil; cling to what is good. Be devoted to one another in brotherly love. Honor one another above yourselves.

Ephesians 4:1-3
As a prisoner for the Lord, then, I urge you to live a life worthy of the calling you have received. Be completely humble and gentle; be patient, bearing with one another in love. Make every effort to keep the unity of the Spirit through the bond of peace.

Ephesians 4:29
Do not let any unwholesome talk come out of your mouths, but only what is helpful for building others up according to their needs, that it may benefit those who listen.

Galatians 6:7-9
Do not be deceived: God cannot be mocked. A man reaps what he sows. The one who sows to please his sinful nature, from that nature will reap destruction; the one who sows to please the Spirit, from the Spirit will reap eternal life. Let us not become weary in doing good, for at the proper time we will reap a harvest if we do not give up.

Philippians 2:3-4
Do nothing out of selfish ambition or vain conceit, but in humility consider others better than yourselves. Each of you should look not only to your own interests, but also to the interests of others.

Colossians 3:12-15
Therefore, as God's chosen people, holy and dearly loved, clothe yourselves with compassion, kindness, humility, gentleness and patience. Bear with each other and forgive whatever grievances you may have against one another. Forgive as the Lord forgave you. And over all these virtues put on love, which binds them all together in perfect unity.
Let the peace of Christ rule in your hearts, since as members of one body you were called to peace. And be thankful.

Galatians 5:22-23
But the fruit of the Spirit is love, joy, peace, patience, kindness, goodness, faithfulness, gentleness and self-control.

Galatians 5:25-26; 6:2
Since we live by the Spirit, let us keep in step with the Spirit. Let us not become conceited, provoking and envying each other.
Carry each other's burdens, and in this way you will fulfill the law of Christ.

command to love your neighbor as yourself? How would family life change? What would happen if you were to make a commitment to raise some of your 'Family Love Review' ratings by at least two numbers in the weeks ahead?

"God's ultimate act of compassion was to sacrifice his Son. By his compassion, we can see the importance of caring for one another. If we follow this model, we must recognize the value of each individual to ourselves and God and operate with godlike compassion."

Close the session by asking one family member to pray for each person in his or her family. Remind families to set up a time for "Table Talk."

Table Talk

Instructions: "Table Talk" offers your family an opportunity to continue discussing the issue studied in class. Set aside 30 minutes for this family time.

But before you begin, remember one important thing: Practice listening as well as talking. Arguments, defensiveness, put-downs or shouting don't encourage conversation.

Now go ahead. Complete the following activity and make new discoveries about yourself and the other members of your family.

Our family "Table Talk" time this week will be _____ TIME _____ DAY

In the space provided, draw a picture of the most compassionate person you know outside your family. List his or her personal qualities that made you come to that conclusion. Don't tell anyone whom you have chosen.

Most Compassionate Person I Know

Personal Qualities

1.
2.
3.
4.
5.
6.
7.
8.
9.

After everyone has finished, show your drawing to the rest of your family to see if they can guess who he or she is. Read the list of "Personal Qualities." If no one guesses, tell your family who this compassionate person is. Your family may never have met this person, so it will be your chance to introduce them to someone special.

Look back at the "Paul's Building Blocks of Compassion" worksheet. Choose a scripture passage and underline all the words or phrases you think are particularly important or say something about how people should treat one another. Share your findings with the rest of your family.

After discussing all of these compassionate qualities, write each family member's name in the following form and list two compassionate qualities you see in that person such as caring, accepting, never critical and so on. Share your responses with the rest of your family.

Family Member	Compassionate Qualities
1.	a.
	b.
2.	a.
	b.
	a.
	b.
	a.
	b.
	a.
	b.
	a.
	b.
	a.
	b.

Share your score from your "Your Emotional Thermometer" worksheet with your family. Discuss what you have learned about yourself from that survey and from your family's surveys. Rate your family on the current level of compassion you feel within your home. Use a scale of 1 to 10 (1 = low compassion; 10 = high compassion). Talk about your reasons for rating the family as you did.

Discuss specific things your family can do to give your home a more compassionate atmosphere. List things each of you can do to make sure family members know they are loved and cared for.

1. One place to start is to make sure each family member gets at least seven hugs a day!
2.
3.
4.
5.

Ask each person to share the last time he or she experienced compassion from other family members. Celebrate these caring moments by closing with sentence prayers.

"Let's Talk" Questions

Instructions: Use these questions to stimulate family discussion throughout the week. An ideal time is right after dinner.

1. Is it hard to show compassion to people you don't like? Why or why not?

2. What is the most important compassionate attitude you want others to extend toward you?

3. Why are hugs important?

4. What would happen in our world if everyone took compassion seriously?

5. In what area of your life do you need compassion the most?

Communicating: Vitamins to Healthy Families

Communication suffers when misinterpretations, assumptions and silence tangle the lines. Family members can learn to untangle the lines of communication by sharing their thoughts and feelings in an honest, open, compassionate way.

This session highlights ways parents and junior highers can improve communication. It explores the biblical foundation for honest conversation and affirms God's call to each of us to keep talking in a Christlike way.

Objectives

During this session participants will:

● list ways they build up or tear down communication in the family.

● explore biblical wisdom for good communication.

● share reasons why parents and young people stop talking to each other.

● make decisions for improving communication in the family.

Biblical Foundation

Communication tips: Proverbs 10:32; 11:12; 12:1, 18, 23; 14:3, 17, 29; 15:1, 7, 12, 23, 28; 16:2, 18, 21, 23, 24, 28, 32; 17:10, 14; 18:4, 8, 13; 19:20; 20:5, 20; 21:14; 22:10

Background for Leader

Families shut and bolt "conversational doors" when they rely solely on assumptions to determine other members' thoughts or feelings. When prejudices color those assumptions, parent-junior higher relationships may wither into silence.

Helping families learn how to communicate is important. Many families often fail to follow the biblical blueprint of tactful and attentive communication. This failure results in conflict and non-productive battles of ego and will.

During the meeting describe several communication techniques such as the following:

1. Listen to the other person. Don't simply wait for your turn to talk.

2. Keep a posture of patience during the conversation.

3. Empathize.

4. Avoid being judgmental, defensive or critical.

5. Ask for clarification when you don't understand a statement.

6. Express your feelings by starting a sentence with "I" rather than "you."

Preparation

Gather empty boxes of various sizes, red construction paper, two rolls of tape, one marker for each person, newsprint and children's wooden building blocks.

Title a sheet of newsprint "Communication Roadblocks" and tape it to a wall.

Cut the red construction paper into brick-sized pieces (approximately 4×7). Make enough so each person has several bricks.

Divide the wooden blocks into two identical piles of various shapes.

Down the center of the room, build a wall from the empty boxes.

Session

Opening (10 minutes)—As people arrive they will find a wall of boxes down the center of the room. Place all junior highers on one side of the wall and parents on the other side. Give each group one marker for each person, one roll of tape and a supply of brick-sized construction paper.

Say: "This wall represents roadblocks to family communication. In the next five minutes I would like each group to think of bricks that build walls in family communication. In other words, what stops us from communicating with each other? For example, kids might write, 'Parents always feel they have to be right.' Parents might write, 'I feel shut out when I get the silent treatment.' Write one idea per brick and tape it to the wall of boxes."

After five minutes, stop the process and discuss the ideas. Write these ideas on the newsprint titled "Communication Roadblocks." Leave the wall in place for the rest of the session.

Theme presentation (5 minutes)—Talk briefly about the theme for the day—building quality family communication. Highlight the communication techniques listed in the Background for Leader section.

Exploration (25 minutes)—Tell the group you are going to conduct a "block experiment." Ask for one parent and one junior high volunteer, then give these instructions: "I would like the two volunteers to sit on the floor in the center of the room with your backs to each other. Everyone else gather in a circle around them."

In front of each volunteer place an identical pile of wooden blocks. Say: "One of you will be the talker in this experiment, one the listener. The talker will build a structure with his or her blocks. While the talker builds, he or she must communicate to the other person all the necessary information to duplicate his or her structure. At no time can the listener ask for clarification or turn around to look. During this round the parent is the talker, the junior higher is the listener. Begin." Instruct the observers to remain quiet and simply watch. When the volunteers finish, have them turn around and compare their creations. Do not discuss what happened.

Ask for two more volunteers, one junior higher and one parent. The junior higher will be the talker, the parent the listener. Say: "Proceed as in the last round except the listener can now tap a block on the floor when he or she needs clarification on instructions. The talker then must attempt to clarify the instructions." Conduct the round. Let the volunteers compare their creations but do not debrief.

Ask for another pair of volunteers to sit back to back. The parent is the talker, the junior higher is the listener. Say, "Proceed as before except this time the listener can ask the talker any question." Conduct the round and then ask volunteers to look at their creations. Debrief the experiment by asking these questions:

1. How do the volunteers feel about this experience?

2. What was frustrating?

3. What happened when your frustration level began to rise?

4. What did the rest of the class observe during this process?

5. After viewing and participating in the block experiment, what are some important conclusions you can make about communication?

Explain: "People don't always understand us even when we're sure we've communicated clearly. When our frustration rises we tend to become less clear in our communication and simply operate on assumptions. Clear communication means talking, listening and asking questions when you don't understand."

Response (10 minutes)—Say: "The first thing we did today was look at communication roadblocks. We just experienced some of the realities and frustrations of communication. Now we are going to look at some communication tips from Proverbs. Turn to the 'Communication Cues From Proverbs' worksheet. Let's take turns going around the room reading them aloud. Put a star by any of the ones you like the best."

Divide into separate groups of junior highers and parents. Ask them to go back to the wall and gather on the opposite sides from where they started. Junior highers will stand on the parents' side, and parents will stand on the junior highers' side. Ask them to think of things they do in their families to maintain open, quality communication. Say: "Take a construction paper brick from the wall, read what it says, turn it over and write a way to overcome that communication barrier. For example, a junior higher could read

Communication Cues From Proverbs

Instructions: Read these cues aloud. Place a star by the ones you find extra meaningful.

14:17—A quick-tempered man does foolish things, and a crafty man is hated.

20:5—The purposes of a man's heart are deep waters, but a man of understanding draws them out.

12:23—A prudent man keeps his knowledge to himself, but the heart of fools blurts out folly.

15:1—A gentle answer turns away wrath, but a harsh word stirs up anger.

22:10—Drive out the mocker, and out goes strife; quarrels and insults are ended.

16:2—All a man's ways seem innocent to him, but motives are weighed by the Lord.

15:23—A man finds joy in giving an apt reply—and how good is a timely word!

16:24—Pleasant words are a honeycomb, sweet to the soul and healing to the bones.

10:32—The lips of the righteous know what is fitting, but the mouth of the wicked only what is perverse.

11:12—A man who lacks judgment derides his neighbor, but a man of understanding holds his tongue.

15:12—A mocker resents correction; he will not consult the wise.

16:32—Better a patient man than a warrior, a man who controls his temper than one who takes a city.

16:18—Pride goes before destruction, a haughty spirit before a fall.

the brick that says, 'I feel shut out when I get the silent treatment.' He or she could write on the back, 'I should always keep sharing and not give the silent treatment.' An adult could read the brick that says, 'Parents always feel they have to be right.' He or she could write on the back, 'When I make a decision I should always explain my reason for it.' "

After seven minutes, collect the bricks from both groups. Talk about their ideas and write them on newsprint.

Closing affirmation (5 minutes)—Gather in family

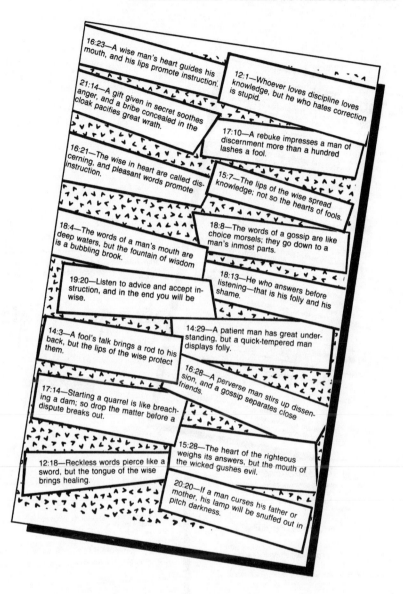

16:23—A wise man's heart guides his mouth, and his lips promote instruction.

12:1—Whoever loves discipline loves knowledge, but he who hates correction is stupid.

21:14—A gift given in secret soothes anger, and a bribe concealed in the cloak pacifies great wrath.

17:10—A rebuke impresses a man of discernment more than a hundred lashes a fool.

16:21—The wise in heart are called discerning, and pleasant words promote instruction.

15:7—The lips of the wise spread knowledge; not so the hearts of fools.

18:4—The words of a man's mouth are deep waters, but the fountain of wisdom is a bubbling brook.

18:8—The words of a gossip are like choice morsels; they go down to a man's inmost parts.

19:20—Listen to advice and accept instruction, and in the end you will be wise.

18:13—He who answers before listening—that is his folly and his shame.

14:3—A fool's talk brings a rod to his back, but the lips of the wise protect them.

14:29—A patient man has great understanding, but a quick-tempered man displays folly.

16:28—A perverse man stirs up dissension, and a gossip separates close friends.

17:14—Starting a quarrel is like breaching a dam; so drop the matter before a dispute breaks out.

15:28—The heart of the righteous weighs its answers, but the mouth of the wicked gushes evil.

12:18—Reckless words pierce like a sword, but the tongue of the wise brings healing.

20:20—If a man curses his father or mother, his lamp will be snuffed out in pitch darkness.

groups and ask members to complete this statement: "One thing I will do to help improve communication in my family is . . ."

Close by saying: "God calls each of us to be open, honest and fair in our conversations with one another. He doesn't want walls to separate us." Then lead the group in tearing down the wall of boxes.

Remind families to schedule this week's "Table Talk" time. Encourage them to keep communication open, honest and filled with compassion.

Table Talk

Instructions: "Table Talk" offers your family an opportunity to continue discussing the issue studied in class. Set aside 30 minutes for this family time.

But before you begin, remember one important thing: Practice listening as well as talking. Arguments, defensiveness, put-downs or shouting don't encourage conversation.

Now go ahead. Complete the following activity and make new discoveries about yourself and the other members of your family.

Our family "Table Talk" time this week will be

_____
TIME
_____
DAY

Think back to the block experiment. Talk about your experiences. What communication issues were raised during that process? Gather some wooden blocks and try the same experiment with different family members.

In the following form write each family member's name. Beside each name write the number of minutes you spend in quality conversation with him or her each week. Quality communication means time spent sharing concerns, interests, ideas, problems, etc.

Family Member	Number of Quality Minutes

Share responses. Is the time spent with each member more than you expected? less? What are some reasons for the times given? Are you surprised? Explain. What improvements do you need to make?

Let's Talk Questions

Instructions: Use these questions to stimulate family discussion throughout the week. An ideal time is right after dinner.

1. What would happen in the world if every nation would openly communicate with each other?

2. What is the one thing that keeps you from sharing your true thoughts and feelings?

3. When people don't talk to one another, what's the outcome?

4. What are three things you wish your family would talk about more?

5. Why is it sometimes easy to discuss opinions but so hard to discuss feelings?

What were some of the communication roadblocks you remember from the session? Write three roadblocks to communication you see in your family.

Roadblock #1   Roadblock #3

Roadblock #2

Share responses. How can you collapse some of those roadblocks? On a scale of 1 to 10 (1 = low; 10 = high), rate the level of open communication in your family.

1   2   3   4   5   6   7   8   9   10

On a scale of 1 to 10 (1 = low; 10 = high), rate your effort in keeping communication open in your family.

1   2   3   4   5   6   7   8   9   10

Share responses and reasons. What do you need to do to improve your communication?

Review "Communication Cues From Proverbs." Choose four favorite passages on which your family can build a communication plan. Use those proverbs to help you complete this statement:

Our family plan to develop better communication with one another will be: _____

_____.

Compare and compile your statements into one family plan. Write it on a separate piece of paper and tape it to the refrigerator. Read your plan daily as a reminder to keep communication open in your family.

God's Promises for His Family

*H*ow good is a promise? In human terms, a promise is only as good as the character of the person making it.

How good is a promise? In God's terms, a promise is as sure as the sunrise, as constant as time and as far-reaching as the universe.

The past 12 sessions focused on God's promises for the family. This session affirms those promises and calls each person to explore the truth that God's steadfast love provides the basis for all relationships. Applying this truth in family relationships builds bridges of warmth, love, affirmation and faith.

Objectives

During this session participants will:

● affirm some of the discoveries they've made in the past 12 sessions.

● explore biblical foundations for God's promises to them.

● make commitments for sharing God's promises with their families.

Biblical Foundation

God promises his strength and safety: Psalm 18:30-33; Isaiah 40:28-31; Philippians 4:12-13

God promises his protection from fear: Psalm 27:1; 121

God promises his help in times of trouble: Psalm 46:1-3; 91:1-6; John 16:33

God promises his love: Psalm 63:3-4; John 3:16-17; Romans 8:35-39

God promises his peace: Psalm 85:8; John 14:27; Philippians 4:6-7

God promises his faithfulness: Psalm 89:1-2

God promises his forgiveness: Psalm 103:1-18; 1 John 1:8-9

God promises his guidance: Psalm 119:1-5; Proverbs 3:1-6

God promises his presence: Psalm 139:1-6; Matthew 28:16-20

God promises his salvation: Romans 10:9-10; Ephesians 1:7-8; 2:4-5

Background for Leader

Dull, dull, dull. Life would be plain and dull without an occasional promise whetting people's appetites. Ears and emotions peak when others make a promise. Promises that offer more adventurous opportunities particularly spark interest.

Promises are frustrating experiences when they're broken or left unclaimed. How disappointing to get excited about a scheduled experience only to have the maker break his or her word. A series of unkept promises erodes trust levels. Likewise, personal failure to follow through on promises is hard on other people.

Broken promises in human experiences often distort understanding and belief in *God's* promises. Rather than use God's commitment as a basis for personal commitment to others, individuals allow disappointment with human promises to determine their commitment to God.

Parents and children can find great hope and guidance in God's promises. Using those promises as relational building blocks, they can create new levels of commitment between each other.

Preparation

Gather Bibles, markers or crayons, masking tape, pencils, several sheets of four colors of construction paper, and one helium-filled balloon for each participant.

Helium for balloons can be obtained from medical suppliers, balloon suppliers or welding suppliers. If you can't get helium, use balloon sticks. Bright-colored, large balloons with "Love" printed on them can be ordered from: Recreation Novelty, 221 Park Ave., Baltimore, MD 21101.

Fill the balloons just before this session. (Helium-filled balloons quickly go limp.) Arrange for a volunteer adult to bring them into the class at your signal.

Arrange chairs in a circle. Set up four tables in the room. On each table, place several sheets of one color of construction paper and markers or crayons. Tape one of the following questions to the center of each table: "What was a recent promise someone made to me?" "What was a recent promise I made to someone?" "What promise made to me was recently broken?" "What promise did I make that I have recently broken?"

Session

Opening (10 minutes)—When participants arrive, explain the opening activity: "This activity will help you think about promises. Each of the four tables has one question taped to it. Go to one of the tables, read the question, then record your answer on the construction paper and keep it with you. Continue this process until you've answered the question on each table."

When participants finish, ask them to sit down. Go around and ask for their responses to some of the questions. Ask them to look through their answers on the construction paper. Ask: "How do you feel when you make and keep a promise? How do you feel when someone keeps a promise to you? How does it feel when a promise to you is broken?"

Theme presentation (5 minutes)—Say: "Today's session is the last one in our time together. We will conclude our experiences by looking at the importance of promises in our lives and some of God's promises for each of us and for our families."

Ask the group to turn to "Promise Packages." These packages contain the scriptures that highlight God's various promises to us.

Exploration (10 minutes)—Distribute Bibles. Divide the

class into mixed groups by asking parents and young people who are sitting closest together to form small groups. Assign two or three packages to each small group. Ask each group to decide on the kind of promise described in each assigned passage.

After a few minutes, bring the groups back together and have them share their insights. Refer to the Biblical Foundation for a description of these promises.

Say: "These promises from God are absolute. They do not change. You can't earn them. They are unconditional gifts of God's amazing grace. You will never have to doubt their availability to you."

Response (15 minutes)—Ask people to turn to "Balloon Brighteners." On that sheet are several balloons. Tell the group: "Think for a moment about the promises of God you just discovered. Think about how these promises could brighten the lives of people you know, especially those in your own family. Pick some of those promises (safety, strength, protection, forgiveness, peace, salvation, love, presence, guidance or help in times of trouble) and fill in the balloons with 'promise brighteners' to share with those around you. For example, 'As I think about God's promise of forgiveness, I promise to see Jim this week and deal with the time he really hurt me.' "

Break the group into family units. Have members complete their worksheets then share their responses.

Bring the group back together and ask for reflections or feelings on putting God's promises into practice toward others.

Closing affirmation (15 minutes)—Say: "The last few weeks have been special for us. We made important insights into our relationships. We shared a lot together. We made an effort to listen to each other. We grew in our understanding and appreciation of one another. As we draw this study to a close, let's spend the remainder of our time looking at how we have grown." Ask:

1. What part of the study has helped your family the most?

2. What have you discovered about yourself?

3. What new appreciations do you have for other family members?

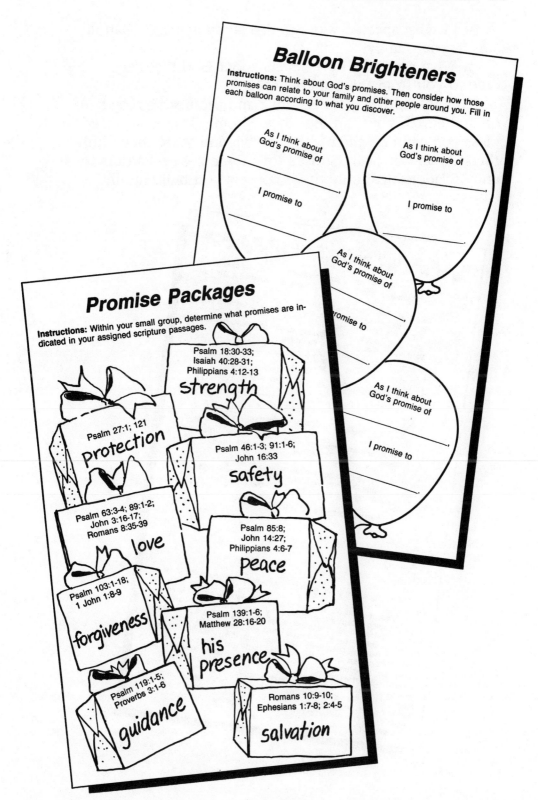

Balloon Brighteners

Instructions: Think about God's promises. Then consider how those promises can relate to your family and other people around you. Fill in each balloon according to what you discover.

As I think about God's promise of

_____

I promise to

_____

As I think about God's promise of

_____

I promise to

As I think about God's promise of

_____

promise to

_____

As I think about God's promise of

_____

I promise to

_____

Promise Packages

Instructions: Within your small group, determine what promises are indicated in your assigned scripture passages.

Psalm 18:30-33;
Isaiah 40:28-31;
Philippians 4:12-13

strength

Psalm 27:1; 121

protection

Psalm 46:1-3; 91:1-6;
John 16:33

safety

Psalm 63:3-4; 89:1-2;
John 3:16-17;
Romans 8:35-39

love

Psalm 85:8;
John 14:27;
Philippians 4:6-7

peace

Psalm 103:1-18;
1 John 1:8-9

forgiveness

Psalm 139:1-6;
Matthew 28:16-20

his presence

Psalm 119:1-5;
Proverbs 3:1-6

guidance

Romans 10:9-10;
Ephesians 1:7-8; 2:4-5

salvation

4. In what specific way has this study affected relationships in your family?

5. What are some new beliefs about God that have come to you from this experience?

Say: "God loves you. His love and promises strengthen you and enrich your life. But these promises have no value unless you embrace them as your own and share them with others. In and through Christ's love there are no barriers to family relationships; only those barriers you build around

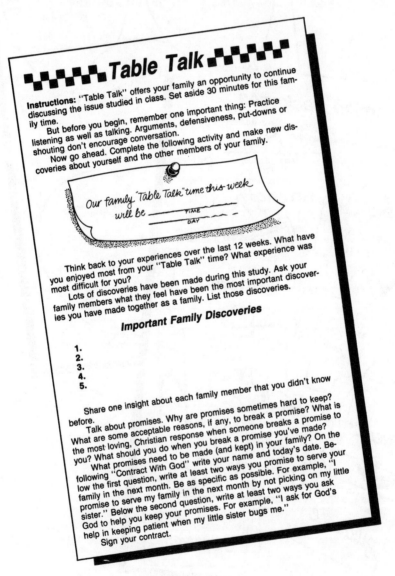

Table Talk

Instructions: "Table Talk" offers your family an opportunity to continue discussing the issue studied in class. Set aside 30 minutes for this family time.

But before you begin, remember one important thing: Practice listening as well as talking. Arguments, defensiveness, put-downs or shouting don't encourage conversation.

Now go ahead. Complete the following activity and make new discoveries about yourself and the other members of your family.

Our family "Table Talk" time this week will be _____
TIME
DAY

Think back to your experiences over the last 12 weeks. What have you enjoyed most from your "Table Talk" time? What experience was most difficult for you?

Lots of discoveries have been made during this study. Ask your family members what they feel have been the most important discoveries you have made together as a family. List those discoveries.

Important Family Discoveries

1.
2.
3.
4.
5.

Share one insight about each family member that you didn't know before.

Talk about promises. Why are promises sometimes hard to keep? What are some acceptable reasons, if any, to break a promise? What is the most loving, Christian response when someone breaks a promise to you? What should you do when you break a promise you've made?

What promises need to be made (and kept) in your family? On the following "Contract With God" write your name and today's date. Below the first question, write at least two ways you promise to serve your family in the next month. Be as specific as possible. For example, "I promise to serve my family in the next month by not picking on my little sister." Below the second question, write at least two ways you ask God to help you keep your promises. For example, "I ask for God's help in keeping patient when my little sister bugs me."

Sign your contract.

yourself." Signal to your volunteer to bring in the inflated balloons.

Say: "These balloons remind us of our journey together. We have been uplifted. We have laughed and we have sighed together. God's promises are the balloons of our lives. Take these and go gladly from this place and live as families of God's promises."

Remind families to schedule their "Table Talk" time for the upcoming week. Encourage parents and young people to continue talking even though this study is complete.

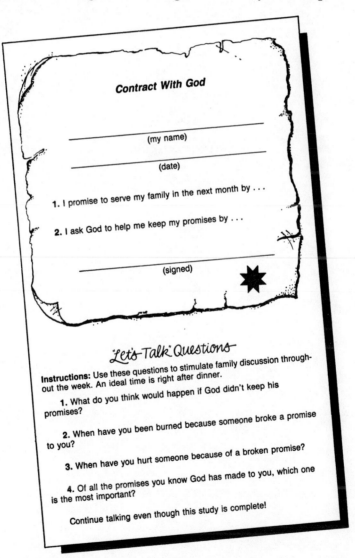

Contract With God

_____
(my name)

_____
(date)

1. I promise to serve my family in the next month by . . .

2. I ask God to help me keep my promises by . . .

_____
(signed)

"Let's Talk" Questions

Instructions: Use these questions to stimulate family discussion throughout the week. An ideal time is right after dinner.

1. What do you think would happen if God didn't keep his promises?

2. When have you been burned because someone broke a promise to you?

3. When have you hurt someone because of a broken promise?

4. Of all the promises you know God has made to you, which one is the most important?

Continue talking even though this study is complete!

Effective Youth Ministry Resources From

Instant Programs for Youth Groups 1, 2 and 3 from the editors of Group Publishing

Get a wealth of ready-to-go meeting plans. Each book includes at least 17 **Instant Programs for Youth Groups**—loads of meeting plans and ideas that interest kids most . . .

Volume 1 — Self-Image, Pressures, Living as a Christian
Volume 2 — Me and God, Responsibility, Emotions
Volume 3 — Friends, Parents, Dating and Sex

Each book comes with loads of ready-to-copy worksheets to involve and interest kids. Order all three—and have a year's supply of ready-to-use meeting plans at your fingertips. What a time-saver!

Paperback, approx. 100 pages (each)
Volume 1—ISBN 0931-529-32-8
Volume 2—ISBN 0931-529-42-5
Volume 3—ISBN 0931-529-43-3

Controversial Topics for Youth Groups by Edward N. McNulty

Get essential tools for teaching your young people how to deal with tough topics. You'll get lots of creative programming ideas for handling difficult subjects. Abortion. Reincarnation. AIDS. Genetic engineering. Christians in politics. Religion and government.

You'll get 40 dynamic programs to spark discussion and help teenagers clarify their own thinking on the hard issues of faith.

Paperback, approx. 360 pages
ISBN 0931-529-51-4

Youth Ministry Care Cards

Your members will love receiving these crazy, colorful, original post cards. Help your kids remember meeting nights and special events by sending **Youth Ministry Care Cards**. Get your message across—"We need you" "You're important" "Great job" "Happy Birthday!" "Get well soon"—in clever, kid appealing ways.

Get both packs—Affirmations and Attendance Builders. Each pack contains 30 cards (6 different designs in each). Turn any day into a special day for your group members when you send out **Youth Ministry Care Cards**!

ISBN 0931-529-36-0 (Attendance Builder Post Cards)
ISBN 0931-529-28-X (Affirmation Post Cards)

Youth Ministry Clip Art Calendar

Spice up your publicity with your fun-to-use **Youth Ministry Clip Art Calendar**. You'll get a full year of calendar sheets for the school year (August-July), all bordered, numbered and ready to use. The work's done for you. You just write in birthdays, meeting times, and special reminders. Then add graphics—choose from scads of camera-ready clip art to paste and copy.

Send calendars home with kids, put them in your newsletter, or post them around your church. Watch interest grow and communication improve when you use this handy calendar-making kit.

Resource kit, 32 pages
ISBN 0931-529-40-9

Involving Youth in Youth Ministry by Thom and Joani Schultz

Develop your young people as leaders with this practical approach to youth ministry. **Involving Youth in Youth Ministry** helps you teach your young people to plan and carry out their own programs and activities. Under your guidance, they'll learn valuable skills. Planning. Self-discipline. Time management. Problem-solving and more. You'll develop a more powerful and effective ministry as you help your kids take charge.

Paperback, 204 pages
ISBN 0931-529-20-4